With the
California Column

With the California Column

Against Confederates and Hostile Indians
During the American Civil War on
the South Western Frontier

The California Column

Frontier Service During the Rebellion

Kit Carson's Fight With the Comanche and Kiowa Indians

George H. Pettis

LEONAUR

With the California Column
Against Confederates and Hostile Indians
During the American Civil War on the South Western Frontier
The California Column
Frontier Service During the Rebellion
and
Kit Carson's Fight With the Comanche and Kiowa Indians
by George H. Pettis

First published under the titles

The California Column
Frontier Service During the Rebellion; or, a History of Company K, First Infantry,
California Volunteers
and
Kit Carson's Fight With the Comanche and Kiowa Indians

Leonaur is an imprint of Oakpast Ltd

Copyright in this form © 2010 Oakpast Ltd

ISBN: 978-0-85706-413-4 (hardcover)
ISBN:978-0-85706-414-1 (softcover)

http://www.leonaur.com

Publisher's Notes

Contents

Brevet Captain George Henry Pettis

Brevet Captain George Henry Pettis, U.S.V.

Brevet Captain George Henry Pettis was born at Pawtucket, Rhode Island, March 17, 1834; his family removed to the village of Cohoes, New York, in 1837. He attended the public schools in that village until he was twelve years of age, when he entered the office of the *Cataract*, the first newspaper published in that village; in 1849 removed to Providence, Rhode Island, where he followed the occupation of printer until 1854, when he went to California, arriving at San Francisco on June 17 of that year, on the steamer *Brother Jonathan, via* Nicaragua; he was engaged at mining in the vicinity of Garrote, Tuolumne County, from June, 1854, until May, 1858, when he arrived at San Francisco *en route* to Frazer River.

The Frazer River bubble having collapsed, he resumed his occupation as a printer, and was employed on the *Alta California* and *Morning Call*, and held a situation on the *Herald* when President Lincoln made a call upon California for troops. He entered the military service of the United States August 16, 1861, as second lieutenant Company B, First California Infantry, Colonel James H. Carleton; promoted to first lieutenant Company K, same regiment, January 1, 1862, commanding the company nearly all of the time, until mustered out on February 15, 1865, when he was immediately mustered into the service again as first lieutenant Company F, first New Mexico Infantry, Colonel Francisco Paula Abreú.

He commanded Company F until promoted to adjutant of

the regiment June 1, 1865, and was finally mustered out, his "services being no longer required," September 1, 1866, at Santa Fé, New Mexico, by Captain Asa B. Cary, Thirteenth United States Infantry, A. C. M., having served continuously five years and fifteen days. Was in a number of skirmishes with Apache and Navajo Indians; brevetted captain United States volunteers March 13, 1865, "for distinguished gallantry in the engagement at the Adobe Walls, Texas, with the Comanche and Kiowa Indians," November 25, 1864, in which he commanded a section of mountain howitzers mounted on prairie carriages.

This expedition was under the command of Colonel Kit Carson, First New Mexico Cavalry. This engagement took place on the north bank of the Canadian River, in the "pan-handle" of Texas, near the boundary-line of the Indian Territory, and lasted from break of day until night. The forces of Carson consisted of about one hundred and fifty California and New Mexican cavalry, with the two gun-detachments of twenty-six men, while the enemy numbered over five thousand of the best Comanche and Kiowa warriors.

Colonel Carson reiterated until the day of his death that "if it hadn't bin for them 'spiritual case' of Pettis's not a man of the expedition would have escaped from the valley of the Canadian River on that day." Upon being mustered out of service he located with his family at Los Algodones, county of San Ana, forty-five miles south of Santa Fé, where he established the "Railroad House, No. 444 Broadway," and performed the duties of U. S. Enrage Agent, and a post-office being established at this village, he was appointed postmaster in 1867.

In 1865 he removed from New Mexico to Providence, Rhode Island; was a member of the Common Council from the Ninth Ward from June, 1872, to January, 1876, and a member of the Rhode Island House of Representatives in 1876 and 1877; was boarding-officer of the port of Providence from 1878 to 1885; was marine editor of the Providence Journal from 1885 to 1887; is now sealer of weights and measures and superintendent of street-signs and numbers at Providence, Rhode Island.

Became a member of the Grand Army of the Republic by joining Kit Carson Post, No. 1, Department of New Mexico, in 1868, and joined Slocum Post, No. 10, Department of Rhode Island, by transfer, in 1872, of which post he held the offices of adjutant and chaplain; was a charter member of Arnold Post, No. 4, Department of Rhode Island, in 1 877, of which post he has held the positions of officer of the day and senior vice-commander; was chief mustering-officer, Department of Rhode Island, in 1877 and 1879, and assistant mustering officer in 1890; was a member of the National Council of Administration, and a delegate to the Twentieth National Encampment, held at San Francisco in 1886.

Became a member of the Military Order of the Loyal Legion of the United States, Commandery of California, November 10, 1886. Insignia No. 5065.

He is secretary of the California Veteran Volunteer Association, and secretary of the United States Veteran Association, of Providence, Rhode Island; a member of the Society of California Volunteers of San Francisco, California, and various other societies.

The California Column

George H. Pettis

Contents

The California Column

Immediately after the first Battle of Bull Run, July 24th, 1861, Governor John G. Downey, of California, received from the Secretary of War, Simon Cameron, a communication which said: "The War Department accepts, for three years, one regiment of infantry and five companies of cavalry, to guard the Overland Mail Route, from Carson Valley to Salt Lake City and Fort Laramie." This was the first official action towards organizing troops in California, and it required but a short time to raise the required number of men, and as fast as the companies were mustered in, at the Presidio, near San Francisco, they were transported across the bay, to Camp Downey, near where are now located the railroad shops, eastward of the Mole.

In the meantime the government at Washington had an insane idea of preparing an army, on the Pacific, to be composed principally of regulars, then stationed on the coast, and under the command of General E.V. Sumner, who was in command of the Department of California, then ship them down the coast, to Mazatlan, where they were to disembark, and proceed overland, "to western Texas, and regain the public property in that state, and draw off insurgent troops from Arkansas, Missouri, etc."

This movement was not to General Sumner's taste, although the governor had been directed to organize four more regiments of infantry, and one of cavalry, to take the place of the regular troops that were to go on the Texas raid.

The First Infantry, with the battalion—five companies of the First Cavalry—were being well drilled and disciplined at Camp

Downey, when news was received at Department Headquarters, that the Secessionists in the south part of the state were becoming turbulent, and more outspoken, and on September 17th, General Sumner ordered Colonel Carleton's command to Southern California. The Texas raid was countermanded by the Washington authorities, and an order was issued for all the regulars to be sent by steamer to New York, as soon as they could be relieved by the volunteers, which movement was immediately undertaken.

The First California Infantry, under Colonel James H. Carleton, and the First California Cavalry, under Lieutenant Colonel Benjamin F. Davis, of the First U. S. Dragoons, had arrived at San Pedro, the sea-port of Los Angeles, and had marched some eighteen miles north of that village, and laid out a camp for fifteen companies, near a small creek, about three miles east of where Santa Monica now is, and called it "Camp Latham," in honour of one of the senators from the state. When the order came for the relief of the regular troops, Major Edwin A. Riggs, of the First California Infantry, was sent with several companies, to Fort Yuma. Some of the regulars were at Los Angeles, (at which point Captain Winfield Scott Hancock, afterwards Major General, was on duty as Captain and Assistant Quartermaster), some of the regulars were at San Bernardino, and others were at San Diego. They were, however, all soon relieved, and rendezvoused at San Pedro for shipment, to New York.

The secession element in Southern California, upon the arrival of the volunteers, became less violent, and the effect of their arrival was salutary. On the 20th of October, General E. V. Sumner was relieved of the command of the Department of California, by Colonel George Wright, of the Twelfth U. S. Infantry. Colonel Sumner was lost on the steamer *Brother Jonathan, en route* to Oregon. Some weeks later Colonel Wright was anxious for authority to throw troops into the State of Sonora, and indited several letters to the War Department for this purpose.

November 20th, Colonel Carleton was called to San Francisco for the purpose of proceeding to and taking command of the troops on the overland route *via* Salt Lake City. While there, news was received of the invasion of New Mexico and Arizona, by General S. H. Sibley, with Texas troops. Wright and Carleton consulted on a plan to proceed with a command through Arizona, and attack Sibley on his flank and rear. General Wright made this matter a subject of a communication to the War Department, under date of December 9th, 1861, in which he urged the importance of the movement and its feasibility, and at the same time, he reiterated the necessity of putting troops into Sonora. The latter proposition never received any support from the authorities at Washington, but, the movement through Arizona was immediately approved, and authorized by General McClellan, as soon as it was submitted to him.

About this time, a number of prominent secessionists, who were anxious to go east, and show their devotion to the cause of the rebellion, organized a party in Southern California, and with one "Dan. Showalter" at their head, attempted to get out of the State, but were captured by a detachment of the First Infantry, and were taken, bag and baggage, and landed in Fort Yuma. Although this made a great deal of talk and noise at the time, the persons in sympathy with the rebellion throughout the State announcing that it was an infringement on the constitutional rights of the citizens to molest them when they were quietly proceeding along the highways, but these fellows were caught in the "*chaparral*," a long way from the road or trail, where they were trying to avoid the troops. Their incarceration was approved by the war department.

The movement against the rebels, under Sibley, having been approved, Fort Yuma was made the starting point of the expedition, and troops were forwarded to that place with all promptitude, an intermediate camp having been made at Warner's Ranch, (a point about half way between Los Angeles and Fort Yuma), which was named "Camp Wright," in honour of the General commanding the Department. Supplies were being rapidly pushed forward, both by teams across the Colorado Desert, as well as by water up the Gulf of California, and the Colorado

River.

The "California Column" originally consisted of the First California Infantry, ten companies, under the command of Colonel James H. Carleton; First California Cavalry, five companies, under command of Lieutenant Colonel E. E. Eyre, Lieutenant Colonel Davis having resigned and gone east, and who was killed at Beverly Ford, Virginia, June 9th, 1863; Light Battery A, Third U. S. Artillery, under the command of Lieutenant John B. Shinn, and Company B, Second California Cavalry, under the command of Captain John C. Cremoney. This command contained fifteen hundred men, well drilled, well disciplined, and all eager to show what stuff they were made of.

Later on the Fifth California Infantry, under command of Colonel George W. Bowie, was added, which brought the command up to about 2,350 men, rank and file. The advance guard or detachment, left "Camp Latham" last, and consisted of Company C, Captain McMullin, and K, Captain Nicholas S. Davis, First Infantry, and Company B, Captain Charles A. Smith, and Company G, Captain Hugh L. Hinds, Fifth Infantry, and followed the route of those in the advance, to "Camp Wright."

While these movements of the California troops were being made, General H. S. Sibley had arrived in New Mexico, with about 3,000 men, and had relieved Colonel Baylor from command. Colonel John R. Baylor had arrived in the territory about the 1st of July, 1861, with several hundred men of his regiment, the "Second Texas Mounted Rifles. Confederate States Army," and had announced himself as the Provisional Governor of New Mexico and Arizona.

On July 25th, Major Isaac Lynde, 7th U. S. Infantry. who was in command of Fort Fillmore, which was about three miles east of La Mesilla, and all the Union forces south of the *Jornado del Muerto*, proceeded to attack Baylor's forces at La Mesilla, and after a desultory assault upon the village, he (Lynde) in the most cowardly manner, returned to the adobe walls of Fort Fillmore, having had three men killed, and two officers and four men wounded. On the morning of the 27th, Lynde vacated the fort, and commenced a retreat for Fort Stanton, having over five hundred men well equipped, armed and officered.

As soon as Baylor learned of Lynde's flight, he pursued him, with less than three hundred poorly armed men, and overtaking him near San Agustin Springs, captured the whole party, which consisted of seven companies of the 7th U. S. Infantry, and three companies of the U. S. Mounted Rifles, without firing a shot. About this time, an independent company of rebels was formed under the command of a Captain Hunter, who was ordered to proceed to Tucson, and operate down the Gila River as far as Fort Yuma.

Sibley had, soon after his arrival in the territory, gone up the Rio Grande to find General Canby, as the latter would not go down the river, and finding Fort Craig too strong to attack, had avoided it, and crossed the river to the easterly side within two miles and in plain sight of Craig. His attempting to reach the river again to get water for his men .and stock at Valverde, just above the *Mesa de la Contedera*, brought on the sanguinary struggle at Valverde, which took place on the 21st of February, 1862, and which was precipitated by that gallant soldier and estimable gentleman, Colonel Benjamin S. Roberts, United States Army.

Early in April, the scouts brought in news to Fort Yuma, that the rebels had left Tucson and were on their way down the Gila River, having captured Captain William McCleave and nine of his Company A. 1st Cavalry, who were scouting at White's Mills, near the Pima villages; and sent them as prisoners to the Rio Grande. McCleave was soon paroled and returned to the column. A command under Captain William Galloway, consisting of his own Company I, 1st Infantry, a detachment of Company A, 1st Cavalry, commanded by Lieutenant James Barrett, with Lieutenant E. C. Baldwin, Company D, 1st Cavalry, and a detachment of Company K, 1st Infantry, under Lieutenant Jeremiah Phelan, with two mountain howitzers, were sent out from Fort Yuma, to proceed along the Overland Mail Route, with Tucson as the objective point.

This command reached the Pima villages with no other signs

of the rebels, than a number of burned hay stacks along the way, and in due time started from that point for Tucson. When they were approaching the "Picacho Peak," the Indian scouts brought in information that a detachment of the rebels was in the immediate front. The detachment was ordered to make a wide detour, so as to strike them in the flank, while Calloway, with the main party, were to attack in front. The enemy were not found in the immediate front, but after travelling several miles, on April 15th. 1862, rapid firing was heard in advance, and arriving upon the spot it was found that Lieutenant Barrett had located the rebels picket, and the first intimation they had of results was that Lieutenant Barrett and two men were killed, and three were wounded.

The rebel loss was two men wounded, and three were taken prisoners. The graves of the killed, the Union Lieutenant and the men, may now be seen within twenty feet of the California Southern Pacific Railroad, as it goes through "Picacho Pass." The Union force bivouacked on the ground that night, and the next day, Calloway having lost his head, ordered a return to be made, against the protests of all his officers. This party was met near Stanwix Station by Colonel West and the "advance detachment," and all proceeded forward to the Pima villages.

A permanent camp was established at the Pima villages and an earth work was thrown lip about the flour mill of Ammi White, who had been carried away, a prisoner,, by the rebels a few weeks before. This earth work was named Fort Barrett, in honour of the lieutenant who had been killed in the skirmish at the Picacho Pass. It required several weeks for the "Column" to get to this point, as only detachments of not over four companies could move over the route through Southern California and through the entire length of Arizona, within twenty-four hours of each other, on account of the scarcity of water.

On the 15th of May. Colonel West and his advance detachment moved out of the Pima villages for Tucson. They left the overland route at the Sacatone Station, going *via* White's Ranch, through the *Casas Grandes*, Rattlesnake Springs, and arrived at old Fort Breckenridge, near the confluence of the Gila and San Pedro Rivers, where the American flag was run up again, on the flag staff of the fort, amid the hurrahs of the men, and the field music playing the "Star Spangled Banner."

At this point the Pima Indian herders, who had been employed to drive along the live stock of the command, and some others who had been employed as scouts, refused to go any further, and demanded their pay of the quartermaster. They asserted that the command was too small to take Tucson; that they were greatly outnumbered by the rebels, and besides, there were rifle pits fully manned, more than a mile in length to be overcome. They were allowed to return home.

The command encamped that night in the *Cañon de Oro*. The next day, May 19th, a short march of fifteen miles was made, and the party encamped within ten miles of Tucson. An early reveille on the morning of the 20th, and the command moved forward with a light step. When it had arrived within two miles of the town. Captain Emil Fritz, Company B, 1st Cavalry was sent for ward, the first platoon to make a detour and come in on the east side of the town; the second platoon, under Lieutenant Juan Francisco Guirado, afterwards *aide-de-camp* on the staff of Brigadier General Joseph R. West, in New Mexico, and later in Arkansas and Missouri, since deceased, was to charge in on the north side, while the four companies of infantry were to move directly on the road, and come in at the west side of the town.

The programme was completely carried out, as the three parties came on to the *plaza* of Tucson at the same moment, the cavalry at a charge, and the infantry on the double quick, but found no enemy. In fact, there was no enemy, nor were there any people, the only living things found within the limits of the town, were an unsuspected number of dogs and cats. The rebels, before they had hurriedly left, had publicly announced that the "Abs" would soon take the fair city, which would then be given over to the ravages of a brutal soldiery.

The rebels retreated to the Rio Grande accompanied by a number of *desperadoes*, amongst whom was the notorious

Judge(?) Ed. McGowan, of San Francisco, of "Vigilante Days" fame, who were also rebels at heart, while the Mexican population, men, women and children, started southward for the Sonora line. Good quarters were found here for the troops, and it required two months time, or until July 20th, to get the "Column" assembled here, with food and forage enough to make another start. Everything, except a small amount of wheat, which was purchased of the Pima Indians, was brought by teams from Southern California, *via* Fort Yuma, a distance of several hundred miles.

No forage or food could be had in or about Tucson, and the men could eat nearly as much as the few trains could bring up. No news had been received from the Rio Grande since the column had commenced its march from California. Several express parties had been sent forward to open communications with General Canby, but none had ever returned. On June 15th, a party of three persons, consisting of Sergeant William Wheeling, Company F, 1st Infantry, expressman John Jones, and a Mexican guide named Chaves, left Tucson with dispatches for General Canby, written on tissue paper.

It was afterwards learned that this party was attacked by Apache Indians as they were emerging out of the Apache Pass, on the 18th; Chaves was killed at the first fire and Sergeant Wheeling was seriously wounded, he soon fell from his horse, and was immediately dispatched. Their bodies were afterwards found horribly mutilated, disembowelled and "spread-eagled"— fires having been built over them, and were filled with arrows, after the manner of "John Apache."

Years afterwards the same fate fell to Jones. Jones escaped almost by a miracle, and getting through the Indians, who followed him for a long distance, he succeeded after a ride of over two hundred miles, in reaching the Rio Grande, at Picacho, a small village about five miles above Mesilla. Here he was taken prisoner by the rebels, who brought him before Colonel William Steele, who examined him, took his dispatches, and threw him into jail. He managed, however, to get word to General

Canby that he was there, and that the "California Column" was really coming, an achievement that was considered absolutely impracticable.

On the 21st of June, a strong reconnoitring party of cavalry, under Lieutenant Colonel Eyre, left Tucson for the Rio Grande. After a hard march they arrived at old Fort Thorn on July 4th, which they found abandoned by the rebels. Here he was reinforced by a squadron of the 3rd U. S. Cavalry, under Captain Rowland, and would have proceeded to attack the rebels at Mesilla, but was obliged to forego that pleasure, by peremptory orders from Colonel Chivington, 1st Colorado Volunteers, at Fort Craig, who was in command of the southern military district of New Mexico, and who was acting under General Canby's orders, as Colonel Steele greatly feared he would be overtaken by the California troops, and in his hurried retreat burned a number of his wagons, and destroyed a large amount of ammunition.

The rebel forces were so disheartened and so thoroughly disorganized, that, had they been attacked by even a small force, they would have at once surrendered.

On July 9th Captain Thomas L. Roberts, with his Co. E, 1st Infantry, and Captain Cremoney's Company B, 2nd Cavalry, and two mountain howitzers, under command of Lieutenant William A. Thompson, 1st Infantry, left Tucson for Rio de Sauze, where they were to establish a camp, having with them rations and forage for Colonel Eyre's command, in case they were forced back by the Texans.

When this command reached Apache Pass, (now Fort Bowie), they were attacked by a large force of Apache warriors, under the leadership of "Cochise," the Indians having possession of the water at that point. After a stubborn contest, in which both trails of the mountain howitzers were broken, in elevating the pieces to reach the Indians upon the hill where the spring was, the Indians were forced to retire, with a loss of nine killed, while the troops suffered a loss of two killed and two wounded.

On the 20th of July Colonel West, with Companies B, Captain Valentine Dresher, C, Captain William McMullin, and K, Lieutenant George H. Pettis, 1st Infantry, and Company G, Captain Hugh L. Hinds, 5th Infantry left Tucson for the Rio Grande. On the 21st, a second command, consisting of Lieutenant John B. Shinn's Light Battery A, 3rd U. S. Artillery, and Company A, Captain Edward B. Willis, 1st Infantry and Company B. Captain Charles A. Smith, 5th Infantry, loft Tucson for the same destination, under command of Captain Willis. On the 23rd, Lieutenant Colonel Edwin A. Rigg. with a third command, consisting of Companies I, Captain William Calloway, F, Captain Washington L. Parvin, D, Captain Francis S. Mitchell, and H. Captain Lafayette Hammond all of the 1st Infantry, followed.

Each of these detachments had subsistence for thirty days, with a full supply of entrenching tools. Up to the time of the arrival of the troops at Tucson, the infantry had packed their knapsacks the entire march, a notable achievement, considering the nature of the country—and its lack of resources—through which they had so far marched, and the fearful heat and thirst which they had encountered.

General Orders, No. 10, "Headquarters of the Column from California, dated Tucson, July 17th, 1862," contained the following paragraphs:

10. That every soldier may move forward with a light, free step, now that we approach the enemy, he will no longer be required to carry his knapsack.

11. This is the time when every soldier in this column looks forward with a confident hope that, he, too, will have the distinguished honour of striking a blow for the old Stars and Stripes; when he, too, feels in his heart that he is the champion of the holiest cause that has ever yet nerved the arm of a patriot. The general commanding the 'Column' desires that such a time shall be remembered by all, but more particularly by those who, from their guilt, have been so unfortunate on such an occasion. He therefore orders that all soldiers under his command, who may be held in confinement, shall be at once relieved.

The troops had been in Tucson for two months, from "May 20th, to July 20th. After the first alarm, upon the arrival of the Union troops, scouts were sent forward towards the Sonora line, and the Mexican residents returned to their homes. A number of American *desperadoes* also put in an appearance. A number of these were arrested by General Carleton who, in a letter to General Wright at San Francisco, said, under date of Tucson, June 10th, 1802:

> I shall send to Fort Yuma, for confinement, starting them today, nine of the cut-throats, gamblers, and loafers, who have infested this town to the great bodily fear of all good citizens. Nearly everyone, I believe, has either killed his man or been engaged in helping to kill him.[1]

Sylvester J. Mowry, of Rhode Island, who had been an officer in the U. S. Army, was living near Tucson, at the Patagonia Mine, and being an uncompromising rebel, was arrested, examined by a military commission, was sent down to Fort Yuma at this time. Tucson soon became a cleanly and model town, and the long rest here repaid the command for the many days of previous marching.

General Carleton, with headquarters of the "California Column" arrived at Fort Thorn, on August 7th, and immediately communicated with General Canby. The balance of the "Column" arrived on the Rio Grande in detachments, as they had left Tucson, one day apart, and by the 15th, Mesilla was made the headquarters of the District of Arizona, and had as a garrison companies B, C, B and K, 1st Infantry, and Company A, 5th Infantry. Shinn's Light Battery A, 3rd U. S. Artillery, Companies

---

1. I have always believed that General Carleton wanted me killed, for he put this detachment under my command to escort them to the Pima villages, a distance of nearly two hundred miles, and gave me a cavalry detachment of ton men, the worst disciplined ones I ever met. The first night out, when I was encamped at the "Point of Rocks," an express arrived from Colonel West, then in command at Tucson, in which I was informed that my prisoners had stated before we left that point, that they would never be taken through alive, and cautioning me to be ever on the alert, or I would not get through. Carleton did not send me for the honour. He was much surprised when I returned safe, but not as much as I was.—G. H. P.

A and E, 1st Infantry, B, 5th Infantry, Band D, 1st Cavalry, and B, 2nd Cavalry, were sent as a garrison to Fort Fillmore, opposite to and about three miles from Mesilla. Shinn's battery being shortly afterwards sent to the "Cottonwoods" about 25 miles south of Fort Fillmore, to recruit their horses.

Company A, 1st Infantry, was sent to Franklin, Texas, (now El Paso), to take care of Simeon Hart's flour mill and look out for the "mail carrier" of the rebels—the notorious "Captain Skillman," afterwards killed by Captain Albert H. French, at Spencer's Ranch, near Presidio del Norte, April 15th, 1864, on the Rio Grande, in an attempt to carry the rebel mail into Texas. All the regular troops were soon relieved and sent up to Fort Craig, and the Californians proceeded to Forts Quitman, Bliss, and Davis, in Texas, and hauled up the Union Flag.

The Southern Overland Mail Route had been opened and the United States military posts in Arizona, Southern New Mexico, and Northwestern Texas, had been reoccupied by troops composing the "California Column." General Carleton in his report to Assistant Adjutant General Drum, of the Department of California, under date of September 20th, 1862, said:

> It was no fault of the troops from California that the Confederate forces fled before them. It is but just to say that their having thus fled is mainly attributed to the gallantry of the troops under General Canby's command. That they were hurried in their flight, by the timely arrival of the advance guard of the 'California Column' under Lieutenant Colonel Eyre there cannot be a doubt. The march from the Pacific to the Rio Grande by the 'California Column' was not accomplished without immense toil and great hardships, or without many privations and much suffering from heat and want of water.

★★★★★★

The march of the 'Column from California' in the summer months, across the great desert in the driest season that has been known for thirty years, is a military achievement creditable to the soldiers of the American army; but it would not be just to attribute the success of this march to any ability on my part. That success was gained only by the high physical and moral energies of that peculiar class of officers and men who composed the 'California Column.' With any other troops I am sure I should have failed.

I send you a set of colours which have been borne by this column. They were hoisted by Colonel West over Forts Breckenridge and Buchanan, and over Tucson by Colonel Eyre over Forts Thorn and Fillmore, and over Mesilla. New Mexico; and over Fort Bliss in Texas. They were hoisted by Captain Cremoney over Fort Quitman. and by Captain Shirland over Fort Davis in Texas, and thus again have those places been consecrated to our beloved country.

On the 18th of September, 1862, General Carleton assumed command of the Department of New Mexico, General Canby having been ordered east by the War Department, the "Column" was soon distributed throughout the Department, and active operations commenced against the hostile Indians—the Apaches and the Navajoes. Treason was at a discount in New Mexico, and no treasonable utterances were allowed; when anything of this kind was attempted, it resulted in the person being immediately arrested, confined in the guard house, and tried by a military commission.

The most incorrigible of this class of persons, was Samuel J. Jones, the well known pro-slavery sheriff at Lecompton, Kansas, in 1857 and '58. Upon the advent of Colonel Baylor's forces in 1861, he was the post-sutler at Fort Fillmore, owning a fine estate at Mesilla, and during the rebel occupation of the territory he was constantly in hot water with the rebels, but not on account of political matters, however, as he was an unadulterated fire-eater. After the "Column" arrived in the District of New Mexico, Jones was brought up in the guard-house about once a month upon an average.

When General Carleton assumed command of the Department of New Mexico he relinquished the immediate command of the "California Column" and published the following order:

Headquarters of the Department of New Mexico,
Santa Fe, N. M., Sept. 21st, 1862.

Gen. Orders
No. 85.

In entering upon the duties that remove him from immediate association with the troops constituting the "Column from California," the Commanding General desires to express his grateful acknowledgment of the conduct and services of the officers and men of that command. Traversing a desert country, that has heretofore been regarded as impracticable for the operations of large bodies of troops, they have reached their destination and accomplished the object assigned them, not only without loss of any kind, but improved in discipline, in morale, and in every other element of efficiency.

That patient and cheerful endurance of hardships, the zeal and alacrity with which they have grappled with, and overcome obstacles that would have been insurmountable to any but troops of the highest physical and moral energy, the complete abnegation of self, and subordination of every personal consideration, to the great object of our hopes and efforts, give the most absolute assurance of success in any field or against any enemy.

California has reason to be proud of the sons she has sent across the continent to assist in the great struggle in which our country is now engaged. The Commanding General is requested by the officer who preceded him in the command of this department, to express for him the gratification felt by every officer and soldier of his command at the fact that troops from the Atlantic and Pacific slope, from the mountains of California and Colorado, acting in the same cause, inspired by the same duties, and animated by the same hopes, have met and shaken hands in the centre of this great continent.

(Signed)   James H. Carleton,
Brigadier General U. S.Volunteers, Comm. Department.

During the years of '63 and '64 there were continual reports
that the rebels in Texas were organizing expeditions to retake
New Mexico and Arizona, which required a large force to be
kept in the southern part of the territory. They were, however,
kept busy against the Apaches and skirmishes were numerous,
and the duty very hard on account of long distances between
water. Among the memorable events in 1863, was the taking
of the celebrated Apache chief "*Mangus Colorado*," (The Red
Sleeve) and his being killed by Captain E. D. Shirland's Company C, 1st Cavalry.

The old chief had been taken prisoner in a skirmish, and was
confined in a Sibley tent at old Fort McLean, near the Mimbres
River, in January, 1863. The guard had strict orders that if he attempted to escape, to shoot him.

In the early morning the soldier on guard in rear of the tent,
saw "Mangus" rise up from the tent and started to run. He raised
his carbine, fired, and the scoundrel fell dead in his tracks. He
had committed so many murders and outrages that the question of whether or not he really attempted to escape, was never
satisfactorily settled—probably on the score that "*the only good
Indian is a dead one.*"

The other event was the expedition against the Navajos, under the command of Colonel Kit Carson, and of which Captain
Asa B. Carey, 13th U. S. Infantry, who was since Paymaster General of the U. S. Army but now retired, was chief commissary
of subsistence, was general aid and military adviser, in which
Companies B and D, 1st California Cavalry, and Companies H
and K, 1st California Infantry, took part. Company G, 1st Infantry, Captain Henry A. Greene, established on July 3rd, 1863,
Fort McRea, at the *Ojo del Muerto*, about two miles west of the
Jornado del Muerto, and there the captain gained much credit for
his constant and repeated conflicts with the Indians.

The Navajo expedition, by July, 1864, had been successful

in capturing over 9,000 of the Indians, and they were taken to Fort Sumner, (*Bosque Redondo*) on the Pecos River, about five hundred miles from their own home. These Indians were completely whipped in to subjugation, all of their crops and plantings were destroyed, and all of their stock captured. They were taken back to their old homes in 1868, and they have never been on the war path since. A large number of the "Column" were stationed at Fort Sumner guarding these prisoners.

During the year 1863, there were three commissioned officers killed and four wounded; fourteen enlisted men were killed and twenty-one wounded. Three hundred and one Indians were killed, eighty-seven wounded and seven hundred and three taken prisoners. During 1864 there were the usual number of skirmishes, and the Navajo war was completed.

Some of the "Column" was in the celebrated "Sand Creek Fight," which took place north of the Canadian river near "Bent's Old Fort." Company K, 1st Infantry and Companies D and B, 1st Cavalry, were as far east as Fort Dodge, Kansas, escorting trains'. In Carson's fight with the Comanche and Kiowa Indians, November 25th, on the Canadian River, at the Adobe Walls, the "Column" was represented by detachments from Company B, Captain Emil Fritz, 1st Cavalry, and Company K, 1st Infantry, Lieutenant George H. Pettis. Major William McCleave, 1st Cavalry, was second in command.

During this year there was one commissioned officer killed, and two wounded, six enlisted men killed, and twenty-three wounded. Three hundred and sixty-three Indians were killed, one hundred and forty wounded. Eight thousand and ninety-three were taken prisoners in the Department of New Mexico.

Nine companies of the 1st California Infantry, and the five original companies of the 1st California Cavalry, were discharged in August and September, 1864, their term of service having expired. On January 20th, 1865, John Wilson, the last enlisted man of Company K, the tenth company of the 1st California Infantry, was discharged. On February 15th, Lieutenant George H. Pettis, of said Company K, was mustered out at Santa

Fe, New Mexico, by Captain Asa B. Carey, Thirteenth United States Infantry, Chief Mustering Officer, when the record of the "California Column" ceased.

History

The biographical sketches of officers and enlisted men of the California Column and the photographs accompanying them were furnished by Captain George H. Pettis, at present State Sealer of Weights and Measures of the state of Rhode Island with residence at Providence, and were also obtained from official sources. They are the most complete and the best obtainable at this time and the Historical Society is under great obligations to Captain George H. Pettis for his excellent work and very timely aid in securing them for the archives and publications of the society. The sketches were edited by Max. Frost, treasurer of the society.

James H. Carleton.

Late Brevet Major General United States Volunteers in Command.

James H. Carleton was appointed second lieutenant. First United States Dragoons, October 18, 1839; promoted to be first lieutenant March 17, 1845; promoted to be captain February 16, 1847; breveted major, February 23, 1847, for gallant and meritorious conduct at Buena Vista, Mexico, and was appointed major Sixth United States Cavalry, September 7, 1861. He was commissioned as colonel First California Infantry Volunteers and is recognized by the War Department as having been in the military service of the United States in that grade and organization from August 7, 1861. He was appointed brigadier general of the United States Volunteers April 28, 1862, which appointment he accepted on the same day; was breveted lieutenant colonel and colonel in the regular army March 13, 1865, for meritorious services in New Mexico; breveted brigadier general in the regular army on the same day for gallant and meritorious services in the Northwest and was breveted major general of the United States Volunteers on the same day for meritorious services during the war. He was honourably mustered out of the volunteer service April 30, 1866; was promoted to be lieutenant colonel, Fourth United States Cavalry, July 31, 1866. He died January 7, 1873.

From October 14th, 1861, to May 15, 1862, he was in command of the district of Southern California; thence to August 14, 1862, in command of the Column from California; thence to September 5, 1862, in command of the district of Arizona; thence to September 18, 1862, in command in the field; thence to September 12, 1865, in command of the department of New Mexico; thence to April 30, 1866, in command of the district of New Mexico. This officer stated that he was born in Eastport, Maine, but did not report to the War Department the date of his birth.

The records on file in the War Department concerning this officer are purely of a military character and contain no information relative to this officer prior to his entry into service.

General Carleton also served with his regiment while a captain in New Mexico during the years of 1855, 1856, and 1857, and engaged in numerous skirmishes and expeditions against the Apaches, Navajos and Utes. A few of the old timers still alive in the Territory, (at time of first publication), remember him kindly and speak of him very highly as a gallant and successful Indian fighter.

His army record is one of the best among the officers of the "old army" before the war.

General Carleton was a Free Mason and a member of Montezuma Lodge No. 1 of that order in the City of Santa Fé and was made an Entered Apprentice April 22, 1856, a Fellow Craft

James H. Carleton,
Brigadier General U. S. Volunteers, Commanding.

April 25, 1856, and a Master Mason April 29, 1856, and remained a member of the lodge until his demitted November 24, 1860. Upon his return to Santa Fé as a commanding general of the Department of New Mexico he affiliated with Montezuma Lodge August 1, 1863, and remained a member thereof until his demise.

ASA B. CAREY.

Brigadier General, U. S. Army, Retired.

Is a native of the state of Connecticut, and was appointed to the West Point Military Academy from that state July 1, 1854; breveted second lieutenant Sixth U. S. Infantry July 1, 1858; appointed second lieutenant, Seventh U, S. Infantry October 22, 1858; promoted first lieutenant Thirteenth TL S. Infantry May 14, 1861; appointed captain Thirteenth U. S. Infantry October 24, 1861; appointed major and paymaster October 5, 1867; lieutenant colonel deputy paymaster general March 27, 1895; colonel assistant paymaster general June 10, 1898; brigadier general paymaster general, January 30, 1899; retired from active service July 12, 1899.

While serving in the Seventh U. S. Infantry Lieutenant Carey marched with his regiment from Utah to New Mexico, the march consuming four months, namely: The months of May, June, July and August, 1860. The four months were full of hardships and severe duty as may well be imagined when the conditions of the country through which the regiment marched at that time are taken into consideration.

From April, 1860, to September, 1861, he participated with his company in an expedition against the Navajos in New Mexico and Arizona, under the command of Lieutenant Colonel Edward R. S. Canby, during which the command did much scouting and fighting. After the expedition returned Lieutenant Carey served as depot quartermaster at Albuquerque, then as depot quartermaster at Fort Union during the winter of 1861-62.

In March and April, 1862, he was in command of two com-

ASA B. CAREY,
Brigadier General U. S. Army, Retired.

panies of infantry and a battery of mountain howitzers which command formed a part of the force under the command of Major J. M. Chivington, which attacked the rear guard of the Confederates constituted of Texas volunteers at the battle of Apache Pass, or "Glorieta," March 28, 1862. The battalion under the command of the then Captain Carey captured the rear guard of the Confederates, and destroyed the enemy's train and supplies of every kind.

This brilliant feat of arms compelled the Confederates to retire in a hurry upon their base of supplies in Santa Fe, the capital, about twenty-five miles to the south of Apache Pass. From there the Confederate force under the command of General Sibley retired south towards Texas, and evacuated the northern part of New Mexico. Captain Carey was then ordered back to Fort Union, and resumed duty as depot commissary and quartermaster at that fort.

Upon the creation of the eastern district of New Mexico he was appointed to the command of all the troops in the district, which contained all of the Territory of New Mexico east of the Pecos River, with headquarters at Fort Union.

Indians were plentiful and warlike. A number of successful expeditions by the troops under his command occurred at various dates during the time he was the commanding officer.

He was then assigned to duty as chief quartermaster in the 1863 campaign against the hostile Navajos and Apaches under the command of Colonel Christopher Carson, afterwards brigadier general U. S. Volunteers, and was with General Carson's force until May 1864. He was detailed by General Carson, who had been promoted to brigadier general, to take the first detachment of Navajo prisoners and locate them on the reservation set apart for them at Fort Sumner, on the Pecos River. Part of the time he was also in command of the expeditionary force, in the Navajo campaign, which transported over 9,000 Navajo prisoners, men, women and children from their reservation in western New Mexico and eastern Arizona to their new reservation at Fort Sumner, on the Pecos River.

After the close of the Navajo campaign he served as chief quartermaster of the Department of New Mexico, with headquarters in Santa Fé. During the winter of 1864-65 he was assigned to duty as chief mustering officer for the Department of New Mexico, and in that capacity had charge of the mustering out of all of the U. S. volunteers, consisting of New Mexico Infantry and Cavalry regiments, and California Infantry and Cavalry regiments. After the close of the war ho was ordered to Washington to settle his accounts.

After his appointment as major and paymaster he performed another tour of duty in New Mexico, namely: as chief paymaster of the district of New Mexico, stationed at Santa Fé. This, however, was not as arduous and as dangerous as his tours of duty in Indian campaigns, and against the Confederate forces commanded by General Sibley.

He was stationed in the city of Santa Fé as chief pay-master from 1868 to 1874, and thereafter ordered to duty in the office of the paymaster general in Washington, which closed his military career in the Sunshine Territory.

He was breveted major for conspicuous gallantry at the battle of Apache Pass, March 28, 1862. Also breveted lieutenant colonel for gallant and meritorious services in the war with the hostile Navajo Indians.

Retired by operation of law July 12, 1899, with the rank of brigadier general and paymaster general of the army.

General Carey made a gallant record during his six years of service in this Territory, and justly attained the reputation of a very meritorious officer and able commander. Many of the old soldiers still alive in New Mexico, (at time of first publication), remember him fondly and kindly, at the date of this, March 1st, 1908.

WILLIAM LOGAN RYNERSON.

Late Captain First California Volunteer Infantry and Captain and Assistant Quartermaster United States Volunteers.

William Logan Rynerson was born in Hardin county, Kentucky, a few miles from the birthplace of Abraham Lincoln, the martyred president of the United States, in 1836. He was raised on a farm and in early life engaged in the raising of blooded horses and cattle. In the latter fifties the California fever seized him and he emigrated to the then "Land of Gold," tramping it across the plains and mountains of Nebraska, Utah and Nevada. The hardships were many but he stood them manfully.

He then engaged in mining and for a while managed a butcher shop in one of the mining camps, studying law at the same time.

When the First California Volunteer Infantry was organized at San Francisco he enlisted and was made first sergeant of Company C of the regiment, January 1st, 1862. He was promoted to second lieutenant of Company B, of the regiment, *vice* Second Lieutenant George H. Pettis, promoted, February 5, 1862.

April 16, 1862, he was promoted to first lieutenant of Company B, of the same regiment. He was appointed adjutant of the regiment shortly thereafter and served faithfully and efficiently in that capacity until August 9, 1864, when he received a captaincy in the regiment.

Early in 1865 he was transferred to the staff as captain and assistant quartermaster of volunteers and served as such until mustered out in 1866. Upon his muster out he settled in Mesilla, Dona Ana county, shortly thereafter moving to Las Cruces, the town then started two miles north of Mesilla.

He was admitted to the bar and commenced the practice of law in Las Cruces.

While in Santa Fé, serving as a member of the legislative assembly from the county of Dona Ana, an altercation ensued between him and Chief Justice John D. Slough of the Supreme Court of New Mexico. Judge Slough had been a colonel in command of the regiment of Colorado Volunteers that participated in the Battle of "Apache Pass or Glorieta," March 28, 1862.

Judge Slough and Colonel Rynerson, the latter having since been breveted as colonel of volunteers for gallant and meritorious services during the war, were both fearless and brave men.

WILLIAM LOGAN RYNERSON.
Late Brevet Colonel U. S. Volunteers,
Captain 1st California Volunteer Infantry.

Judge Slough while in the billiard room of the Fonda Hotel, then the principal stopping place and leading *caravansery* between Kansas City and West Port, in Missouri, and San Francisco, California, made very bitter and slurring remarks concerning Colonel Rynerson which were reported to the latter.

In those days everybody who could afford it in the Southwest carried a pistol. Colonel Rynerson went to the Fonda, called upon Judge Slough to retract and as the story goes, Judge Slough instead of doing so endeavoured to put his hand behind his back, to draw a Derringer he carried. At that moment Colonel Rynerson pulled his pistol and shot him dead. This happened on the 15 day of December, 1867.

There was testimony adduced to the fact that Judge Slough had a Derringer pistol in his hand which he put behind his back.

A coroner's jury investigated the affair and fully exonerated Colonel Rynerson. Thereafter Colonel Rynerson became a prominent citizen. He was an influential politician and enjoyed a good practice as a lawyer until the time of his death which occurred July 4, 1893.

He was prominent in the Masonic order and attained the thirty-second degree of Scottish Rite Free Masonry and had served the Grand Lodge of New Mexico as second Grand Master in 1879. He was also a member of Santa Fé Chapter No. 1, Royal Arch Masons and of Santa Fé Commandery No. 1, Knights Templar. He had attained a 32nd degree Master of the Royal Secret, in the Ancient and Accepted Scottish Rite of Freemasonry, for the Southern Jurisdiction of the United States; was a member of the Santa Fé Lodge of Perfection No. 1.

He was a member of the constitutional convention of New Mexico in 1889 and had served several times as territorial district attorney of his district and as a member of the legislative council and the House of Representatives of the New Mexico assembly.

As a man, as a citizen, as an official and as a soldier he made a splendid record. In the Masonic fraternity he assumed a high position on account of his loyalty and zeal as a Free Mason. His remains were buried with Masonic honours in the Masonic cemetery at Las Cruces.

GEORGE HENRY PETTIS.

Brevet Captain United States Volunteers, First Lieutenant Company K, First California Volunteer Infantry.

George Henry Pettis was born at Pawtucket, R. I., March 17th, 1834; at the age of twelve years entered the office of the *Advertiser*, a newspaper published at Cohoes, New York; in 1849 removed to Providence, R. I., where he followed the occupation of printer until 1854, when he went to California, arriving at San Francisco on June 17th, of that year, on the steamer *Brother Jonathan, via* Nicaragua; he was engaged in mining in the vicinity of Garrote, Tuolumne county, from June, 1854, until May, 1858, when he arrived at San Francisco *en route* to Frazer River.

The Frazer river bubble having collapsed he resumed his occupation as a printer, and was employed upon the *Alta California* and the *Morning Call*, and held a situation of the *Herald*. When President Lincoln made a call upon California for troops, he entered the military service of the United States as Second Lieutenant, Company B, 1st California Infantry. He was promoted to First Lieutenant, Company K, same regiment, January 1st, 1862, commanding the company nearly all of the time, until mustered out on February 15th 1865, when he was immediately mustered into the service again as First Lieutenant, Company F, 1st New Mexico Volunteer Infantry, Colonel Francisco Paula Abreú.

He commanded Company F until promoted to adjutant of the regiment, June 1st, 1865, and was finally mustered out, his "services being no longer required," September 1st, 1866, having served continuously for five years and fifteen days. He was in a number of skirmishes with Apache and Navajo Indians; breveted Captain U. S. Volunteers, March 13th, 1865, "for distinguished gallantry in the engagement at the Adobe Walls, Texas, with the Comanche and Kiowa Indians," November 25th, 1864, in which he commanded the Artillery.

CAPTAIN GEORGE H. PETTIS.
First Regiment California Volunteer Infantry.

In 1868, he removed from New Mexico to Providence. R. I.; was a member of the Common Council, from the Ninth Ward, from June, 1872, to January 1876 and a member of the Rhode Island House of Representatives in 1876 and 1877; was "Boarding Officer" of the port of Providence from 1878 to 1885; was marine editor of the *Providence Journal* from 1885 to 1887; Sealer of Weights and Measures and Superintendent of Street Signs and Numbers at Providence, Rhode Island from March 10th, 1891 till 1897. He is now State Senior of Weights, Measures and Balances, of the State of Rhode Island, having been appointed February 1st, 1901, (at time of first publication).

He became a member of the Grand Army of the Republic, by joining Kit Carson Post No. 1, Department of New Mexico, in 1868, and joined Slocum Post, No. 10, Department of Rhode Island by transfer, in 1872, of which post he held the offices of Adjutant and Chaplain; was a charter member of Arnold Post No. 4, Department of Rhode Island, in 1877, of which post he has held the positions of Officer of the Day and Senior Vice Commander; was Chief Mustering Officer, Department of Rhode Island, in 1877 and 1879, and Assistant Mustering Officer in 1890: was a member of the National Council of Administration and a Delegate to the Twentieth National Encampment, held at San Francisco in 1886. Commander of Arnold Post No. 4, Department of Rhode Island, 1897. He was the first president of the "California Volunteer Veterans Association." elected at Detroit, Michigan, August, 1891. and has held the office of Secretary and Treasurer since.

He became a member of the Military Order of the Loyal Legion of the United States, Commandery of California. November 10th, 1886. Insignia No. 5065. He is a member of the Society of California Volunteers: also of the Society of California Pioneers of New England. Is an Honorary Member of the Second Rhode Island Veteran Association; Battery B, Veteran Association; Fourth Rhode Island Veteran Association; and the Fifth Rhode Island, and Battery F, Veteran Association, (at time of first publication).

JOSEPH F. BENNETT.

Brevet Lieutenant Colonel U. S.Volunteers.

The following biographical sketch of this gallant and efficient soldier is taken from the columns of the *Mexican Herald,* published in the City of Mexico, July 9, 1904:

Joseph F. Bennett was born in Putnam County, New York, November 11th, 1830. He received an education afforded by the common schools, and graduated from Millville Academy, Orleans county, New York. In 1849 he accompanied his parents to Janesville, Wisconsin.

In 1858 he emigrated to California and British Columbia, going by the Isthmus of Panama, in which countries he was actively engaged in mining until the breaking out of the war, when on the call of President Lincoln for 5,000 volunteers from California, in August, 1861, Colonel Bennett aided in raising and organizing the First California Infantry Volunteers enlisting as a private in G company of that regiment.

In the winter of 1861 he was made sergeant major of the regiment, and in April 1862, he was commissioned second lieutenant of I company, and assigned by General James H. Carleton as assistant adjutant general of the "Column from California," at his headquarters in Santa Fé, N. M. Upon the recommendation of General Carleton, and General J. R. West, Lieutenant Bennett was commissioned by President Lincoln, captain and assistant adjutant general United States Volunteers, and was assigned to duty as adjutant general of the district of Arizona,

On March, 1864, under orders of the secretary of war, Captain Bennett reported for duty to Major General W. S. Rosecrans at St. Louis, Missouri, thereafter he participated in the Price campaign and invasion of Missouri in the autumn of that year. During this period, Captain Bennett was breveted major and lieutenant colonel on the same day by the president for "gallant and meritorious services."

In May 1865,, Colonel Bennett was sent by General G. M. Dodge, then commanding the department of the Missouri, into Arkansas to offer terms of surrender to Brigadier General M. Jeff

Thompson, Confederate States Army, and received the surrender of General Thompson and paroled his command, numbering about 9,000.

In the summer and fall of 1865, Colonel Bennett accompanied General Dodge in a campaign against the Indians in the Northwest, at the time of the combined uprising of nearly all of the tribes in the western country. In the winter of 1865, at his own request, Colonel Bennett was ordered to report at his home to await his order of muster-out and was mustered out of the service in June, 1866, having served throughout the Rebellion.

Colonel Bennett was afterwards commissioned by President Grant, as vice consul to Chihuahua, Mexico, but, having actively engaged in business in New Mexico, declined that appointment. Colonel Bennett had served in many official capacities in his adopted territory as county clerk, clerk of the United States district court, commissioner of the court of claims, United States commissioner and in 1871-72 was a member of the legislative council. He had been identified with many of the leading enterprises in the territory, both private and public, and in May, 1889, was appointed by President Harrison United States Indian agent for the Mescalero Apaches.

Colonel Bennett was married at Las Cruces, New Mexico, February 4th, 1864, to Miss Lola Patton, of La Mesilla. They had a family of seven children living as the fruit of their union. Colonel Bennett was a Royal Arch Mason and a member of Philip Sheridan Post, G. A. R., Las Cruces, N. M., and served one term as assistant adjutant general of the Department of New Mexico, Grand Army of the Republic.

Colonel Bennett was appointed vice and deputy consul general of the United States in the City of Mexico in September, 1897, and served as such two years.

He was the first member of the new society of the American colony to die since its organization.

CYRUS H. DE FORREST.

First Lieutenant, First Colorado Volunteer Infantry.

Cyrus H. De Forrest entered the service as first lieutenant First Colorado Infantry, and participated with his command in the battle at Apache Pass (or Glorieta) in 1862. He served as *aide de camp* on the staff of brigadier General James H. Carleton with headquarters at Santa Fé during 1863, 1864, 1865 and 1866. He is now living at Cleveland, Ohio, (at time of first publication).

CYRUS H. DE FORREST.

GEORGE S. COURTRIGHT.

Assistant Surgeon U. S. Volunteers.

George S. Courtright served for three years as post surgeon at Fort Sumner on the Pecos River and was stationed there during the time the Navajo Indians were held as prisoners on the Fort Sumner reservation. He was also surgeon for the campaign in the expedition commanded by Brigadier General Christopher Carson ("Kit Carson") against the Comanches and Kiowa Indians and was engaged at the Battle of the Adobe Walls, November 25 1864.

DR. GEORGE S. COURTRIGHT.

Benjamin C. Cutler.

Adjutant, First California Volunteer Infantry.

Benjamin C. Cutler entered the service as adjutant of the First California Volunteer Infantry, August 15, 1861. He served with the regiment in that capacity until he arrived in New Mexico when he was appointed by Brigadier General James H. Carleton commanding the expeditionary force, as assistant adjutant general of the Department of New Mexico with the rank of captain, and continued in that position until 1866. His death occurred shortly thereafter and his remains were interred in the National cemetery in Santa Fé.

Benjamin C. Cutler.

WASHINGTON L. PARVIN.

Captain Company F, First California Volunteer Infantry.

This officer entered the service upon the organization of the regiment at San Francisco, California, August 16, 1861. He resigned November 26, 1862, at Mesilla, Dona Ana county New Mexico. He then returned east and now lives in Washington where for nine years he has been doorkeeper at the War Department, (at time of first publication).

WASHINGTON L. PARVIN.

John L. Viven.

Late Brevet Captain U. S. Volunteers.

John L. Viven entered the service in November, 1861, as a sergeant in Company D, First California Volunteer Cavalry. During most of his service he was on duty as a clerk at the department and district headquarters. He was mustered out at Santa Fé, March 15, 1864, to accept a second lieutenant's commission in the First New Mexico Volunteer Cavalry, and was promoted to first lieutenant March 25, 1865. Honourably mustered out April 19, 1866, at Santa Fé, New Mexico. Was appointed second lieutenant 12th U. S. Infantry February 23, 1866; promoted to first lieutenant April 5, 1866, and appointed regimental quartermaster March 6, 1869, which position he filled to February 28, 1871. Promoted to captain March 31, 1873. Died January 9, 1896. He was breveted captain U. S. Volunteers March 2, 1867, for faithful and meritorious services during the war.

John L. Viven.

J. B. WHITMORE.

Late First Lieutenant First California Volunteer Infantry.

Enlisted August 16, 1861. Immediately appointed sergeant major of the First California Volunteer Infantry. Was appointed second lieutenant of Company A, of the First California Volunteer Infantry, September 5, 1861, and first lieutenant, Company G, First California Volunteer Infantry, October 25, 1862. He was with the company that was ordered to and established Fort McRae at the *Ojo del Muerto*, the "Spring of Death," and which was located in what is now called McRae Canyon. This canyon leading from the *Jornado del Muerto* to the Rio Grande and Fort McRae and the spring are situated about one and one-half miles from the river. There his company did very good service against hostile Apaches. Lieutenant Whitmore was mustered out with the regiment after its completion of service. He committed suicide at Los Angeles, June 21, 1898.

LIEUTENANT J. B. WHITMORE.

JACOB J. REESE.

Sergeant Company C, Fifth California Volunteer Infantry.

Jacob J. Reese served as a sergeant in Company C, Fifth California Volunteer Infantry during his whole term of service. He enlisted in the regiment at its organization in San Francisco and was mustered out after expiration of service in New Mexico. His command was engaged in several skirmishes with the Apaches in which he conducted himself with bravery and coolness. He had all the qualities of a good soldier and was very popular among his comrades. He is now spending his old age in peace and quiet in Harrisburg, Pennsylvania, (at time of first publication).

JACOB J. REESE.

CHARLES H. WALKER.

First Sergeant Company K, First California Volunteer Infantry.

Enlisted at San Francisco, November 22, 1861, and was assigned to Company K, First California Volunteer Infantry. Was promoted to first sergeant of his company, April 28, 1863. Honourably mustered out November 29, 1864. His record as a soldier is first class. He is now living at Globe, Arizona, (at time of first publication). He served with the regiment during its entire campaign at stations in Arizona and New Mexico.

CHARLES H. WALKER.

ARTHUR I. LOCKWOOD.

Corporal Company C, First California Volunteer Infantry.

Enlisted in the regiment at its organization in San Francisco and served with it during its entire service in Arizona and New Mexico. He was a fine soldier.

He is now a resident of San Antonio, Texas, where he has held the office of mayor of the city, and also has been elected several times to the office of alderman, (at time of first publication).

ARTHUR L. LOCKWOOD.

Julius C. Hall.

Enlisted at San Francisco, November 9, 1861, and served his full term of enlistment, being mustered out at Fort Union, New Mexico, November 29th, 1864. He was an exemplary soldier and served with his regiment in Arizona and New Mexico.

He is now a resident of Wallingford, Connecticut, and an honoured and respected citizen enjoying all the comforts of a well spent life, (at time of first publication).

Julius C. Hall.

DAVID DOOLE.

Enlisted in Company A, First Regiment California Infantry at San Francisco, August 15th, 1861. He served his full term of enlistment in the regiment. He was with his company during its campaign in Arizona and New Mexico. He had served before in the regular army in the Sixth U. S. Infantry, and participated in the expedition to Utah in 1860. He is still alive, hale and hearty and a respected citizen of Mason, Texas. He is a member of the Fraternity of Ancient Free and Accepted Masons, and has held the highest positions in the lodge in his home town, (at time of first publication).

DAVID DOOLE.

Frontier Service
During the Rebellion;
or, a History of Company K,
First Infantry,
California Volunteers

George H. Pettis

Contents

Frontier Service
During the Rebellion

The first battle of Bull Run had been fought. The government had become satisfied that the slaveholder's rebellion was not to be put down with seventy-five thousand men. The Union people of the United States now fully realized that the rebels were to use every effort on their part towards the establishment of the Confederacy, and the men of the north, on their part, were ready to "mutually pledge to each other our lives, our fortunes, and our sacred honour" to preserve the government as their fathers before them had pledged themselves to establish it. The loyal States were ready to respond to any demand made upon them by the government, and there were none more anxious to do their duty to the old flag than the Union men of California.

The people of that far distant part of our country were, in the early days of our "late unpleasantness," stirred to their very depths. A large portion of the inhabitants had emigrated from the southern States, and were, therefore, in sympathy with their brethren at home. General Albert Sydney Johnston was in command of the military department, and a majority of the regular officers under him were sympathizers with the rebellion, as were a majority of the State officers.

The United States gunboat *Wyoming*, lying in the harbour of San Francisco in the early part of '61, was officered by open advocates of secession, and only by the secret coming of General E. V. Sumner, who arrived by steamer one fine morning in the early part of '61, totally unknown and unannounced, and presenting himself at the army headquarters on Washington Street, San Francisco, without delay, with, "Is this Gen. Johnston?"

"Yes, sir."

"I am General E.V. Sumner, United States Army, and do now relieve you of the command of this department," at the same time delivering the orders to this effect from the War Department at Washington, were the people of the Pacific States saved from a contest which would have been more bitter, more fierce, and more unrelenting than was exhibited in any part of the United States during all those long four years of the war.

As I have said before, the prompt and secret action of the government and that gallant old soldier, General E. Y. Sumner (for you all will remember that California had no railroads and telegraphs in those days), prevented civil war there. The secessionists, who were preparing to take possession of the property of the government in that department and turn the guns of Alcatraz, Fort Point and the Presidio upon the loyalists, were taken completely aback; they delayed action. General Sumner took all precautions against surprise, and the Union men of the Pacific States breathed free again, for civil war had been driven from their doors. Many of the secession leaders, with General Albert Sidney Johnston, seeing their plans miscarry, left the State shortly after, and did service in the Confederate armies.

On the steamer from the States that brought the news to California of the disaster at Bull Run, came orders from President Lincoln for that State to furnish its quota of men for the Union army. The same afternoon, the Franklin Light Infantry, a militia company, composed of printers only, held a meeting at its armoury on Sacramento Street, and voted unanimously to offer their services to the government, which was accordingly done, and they were the first company that was mustered into the United States service in California, and was afterwards known as Company B, First Infantry, California Volunteers, and were officered as follows: Captain, Valentine Drescher; First Lieutenant, Francis S. Mitchell; Second Lieutenant, George H. Pettis.

Other companies were soon formed, and the regiment,

with nine companies, went into camp of instruction at Camp Downey, near Oakland.

The regiment had been in camp but a few days when it was ordered to proceed by steamer to Los Angeles, in Southern California. The transfer was made, and the regiment went into camp about nine miles from Los Angeles, on the seashore, where the town of Santa Monica now is. The First Battalion Cavalry, California Volunteers, consisting of five companies, under command of Lieutenant Colonel Davis, who was afterwards killed before Richmond, also accompanied us.

In a few days after the establishment of this camp, Lieutenant Pettis, of Company B, was sent on detached duty as recruiting officer to San Francisco, in order that the nine companies now in camp should be filled to the maximum standard. The tenth company had not been admitted to the regiment as yet, although several had made application for the position.

Lieutenant Pettis arrived in San Francisco about the fifteenth of October, and immediately commenced business by opening his recruiting office on the corner of Montgomery and Clay Streets, in the same building with the *Morning Call*. He was successful, as by the fifteenth of January he had recruited and sent to the regiment one hundred and two men, and was ordered by General George Wright, then commanding the department of California (and who was afterwards lost on the steamer *Brother Jonathan* on his way to Oregon) , to close his office and join his regiment at Camp Latham.

In the meantime, four companies of the regiment, under Major E. A. Rigg, had proceeded to Fort Yuma, on the Colorado River, and relieved the regulars who were there. Captain Winfield Scott Hancock, Assistant Quartermaster United States Army, had also been relieved and ordered to the States. He had been on duty at Los Angeles. Three companies of the regiment had been ordered to Warner's Ranch, about half way between Los Angeles and Fort Yuma, and established Camp Wright.

On the twelfth of February, orders had been received by Colonel J. H. Carleton, commanding the regiment, to form the tenth company of his regiment from the recruits enlisted in San Francisco by Lieutenant Pettis. Company K, First Infantry, California Volunteers, was thus formed, and was officered as follows: Captain, Nicholas S. Davis, promoted from First Lieutenant of Company A; First Lieutenant, George H. Pettis, promoted from Second Lieutenant of Company B; Second Lieutenant, Jeremiah Phelan, appointed from Hospital Steward of the regular army.

In the meantime, the government at Washington had received information that General H. H. Sibley had left San Antonio, Texas, with about three thousand seven hundred rebel soldiers for New Mexico, and as the government had immense stores of clothing, camp and garrison equipage, and commissary stores in different posts in that Territory and Arizona, with but few troops to defend them, and a majority of the officers avowed secessionists, the rebels expected an easy conquest. Accordingly, Colonel Carleton had orders to organize what was known as the "California Column," which consisted of the First and Fifth Infantry, California Volunteers, (George W. Bowie was Colonel of the Fifth Infantry, California Volunteers); First Battalion Cavalry, California Volunteers; Company B, Captain John C. Cremoney, Second Cavalry, California Volunteers, and Light Battery A, Third United States Artillery, Captain John B. Shinn.

That an idea may be obtained of the difficulties of this enterprise, I will say that it is about nine hundred miles from Los Angeles to the Rio Grande, not a pound of food or of forage was to be obtained on the route, and everything to be consumed had to be brought from California. Neither was there, as we afterwards ascertained, a single resident in all that long march, except at Fort Yuma. The country through which the "Column" passed was without water, and the Colorado and Gila Deserts to be crossed before we should come in sight of the green cottonwoods of the Rio Grande. The Apache Indians supposed that they had driven all the whites out of the Territory of Arizona, and the former required constant watching and attention. In consequence of the scarcity of water on the route, the "Column" could only be moved in detachments.

66

Companies K and C, First Infantry, and Company G, Fifth Infantry, Captain Hugh L. Hinds, left Captain Latham about the first of March, 1862, under command of Captain William Mc-Mullen, of Company C, and arrived at Camp Wright in due season, it being about one hundred and forty miles. The only incident on this march worthy of mention was, that when the battalion marched through the town of Los Angeles the American flag had been hauled down from the court house.

As it was well known that the people of Los Angeles at that time were nearly all strong in their sympathies with the rebellion, it was thought that the hauling down of the flag was to insult the command. Consequently, on the arrival of the battalion on the banks of the Los Angeles River, which flows on the eastern side of the town, it was halted and Captain McMullen returned, and, finding some of the town officials, insisted that the flag should be hoisted immediately. The citizens denied any intended insult to the flag, and proceeded to replace it, which being seen by the men of the battalion, they gave three cheers, and continued on their way.

A delay of a couple of weeks at Camp Wright, when orders were received by Lieutenant Colonel J. R. West, of the First Infantry, commanding at Camp Wright, to organize the advance detachment of the " Column," to consist of Companies K and C, First Infantry, California Volunteers, and Companies B and G, Fifth Infantry, California Volunteers, and proceed without delay to Fort Yuma. The command as above constituted left camp at a late hour in the afternoon, and after a short march made camp beside a *laguna*, or pond. It rained during the night, and daylight found us at breakfast, which was quickly dispatched, and we were soon on our march, the road continually ascending.

At nine o'clock in forenoon we had reached the line of snow, where it was snowing heavily. At noon we had reached the summit, and found the snow about two feet in depth, and as cold as Greenland. A short halt was made, when great fires were built to warm the men, and then the command moved down the mountain. At three o'clock in the afternoon we passed through the line of snow, shortly after through the precipitous *cañon* of San Felipe, and towards evening went into camp, the grass being more than knee high, the air redolent with the perfume of flowers and the sweet melody of the birds.

A short march the next day brought us to Las Dos Palmas, or the "Two Palms," so called from the fact that two luxuriant palm trees formerly flourished here, the stumps of which were then to be seen. Thence to Carizo Creek, nine miles, where the command rested one day. Here commences the then much-dreaded Colorado Desert. For more than a hundred miles we were at the mercy of its sands and storms and burning sun.

Such another scene of desolation does not exist on the American continent; treeless mountains on either side, brown and sombre to their very tops; no signs of life were to be seen anywhere. Although it was in the first days of April, still the sun poured down with an intensity that I had never before experienced, no shade could be found, and the very water in the creek could not be bathed in—being more fit for cooking than bathing, it being so hot. Such was the Colorado Desert as we approached it. What will it be further on? We shall see.

The command left camp at Carizo Creek in the middle of the afternoon, and continued the march until midnight, when we arrived at Sackett's Wells. Here it was supposed a ration of water for the men would be found, but upon examination it was ascertained that somebody had knocked the bottom out of the well, and no water was to be obtained, except such as could be caught in cups as it trickled drop by drop from the strata of clay that had heretofore formed the bottom of the well. No camp could be made here, and the command moved on, marching until about ten o'clock in the morning, when we arrived at the Indian Wells, having made thirty-two miles.

A large number of the men were now suffering for the want of water, and the animals, upon discovering the green bushes in the distance, near these wells, pricked their ears, and every exertion was required by riders and drivers to prevent a stampede, so much were they in want of water. Upon our arrival it was found that but a few buckets of water was in the well, as a detachment of cavalry had made camp there the day before, and had only left upon seeing our command approach, using all the water in the well for their animals before leaving. However, guards were placed over the well, men sent down to pass the water up as it collected, and in the course of a few hours the men had each received his pint of water; then the animals were furnished.

Before the water had all been distributed, one of those terrible sand storms for which this desert is renowned began, and as the sun went down it was at its very height. Neither man nor animal could face this shower of stones and gravel, and the sand and dust penetrated everything. The only thing that was to be done was to throw oneself down upon his face, draw his blankets around him, and ride it out, sleeping. The storm continued through the night, and before dawn approached it had ceased, and upon crawling out of my sand bank, I saw in all directions what appeared to be graves, but they were only mounds of sand that had been formed by the storm over the bodies of the soldiers. Imagine, if you can, near four hundred of these mounds becoming animate and dissolving in the desert, as reveille sounded.

At about noon the command moved on, and after marching twenty-five miles arrived at Alamo Mucho at about two o'clock in the morning. Here was found a well that would have furnished water for an army corps—sweet, cold water. It was a pleasure to look at this, to hold it in a tin cup, look at it, take a mouthful, holding it there a time before swallowing it; it seemed a sin to drink it. This water was not taken on the point of the bayonet, as water had been taken for the past four days, and we had marched sixty-six miles from Los Dos Palmos since we had our fill of water. After the men had satisfied their thirst they spread their blankets wherever they pleased, and there was no person in that command, except the guard, that was not soon in the arms of Morpheus.

Before daylight another sand storm commenced, and when reveille was beat off, not a dozen men were in line, and they were only brought out of their sand hills by beating the long roll. The storm subsided in the early afternoon, when the command moved on, making Gardiner's Wells, twelve miles, before sundown, where was found a fine well with plenty of water, but none of the command wanted any, the only objection being, and that a slight one, that there was standing above the level of the water in the well, a pair of boots—and a dead man in them. Seven Wells was soon reached, and, as the name implies, there were plenty of wells, but there was no water.

Thence to Cook's Well, twelve miles, with plenty of good water, thence fourteen miles to the Colorado River, at Algodones. The next day, before noon, the command arrived at Fort Yuma and went into camp. Here we met Don Pascual, a head chief of the Yumas, Don Diego Jaeger, and the "Great Western," three of the most celebrated characters in the annals of Fort Yuma.

It was supposed that our command was to constitute the advance of the "Column" from Fort Yuma. But upon our arrival at that point, we found that a reconnoitring party, consisting of Company I, First California Infantry, Captain W. P. Calloway; Company A, First California Cavalry, Captain William McLeave, and Lieutenant Phelan, with detachments for two mountain howitzers, had been sent up the Gila River, as the Indians had reported that a large body of rebels were advancing on Fort Yuma from Tucson.

On the third day after our arrival we crossed over the Colorado River and continued our march. We passed the divide between the Colorado and Gila Rivers, and arrived at Gila City that afternoon, eighteen miles. Our route was the old overland stage route on the south side of the Gila. Here we first saw that peculiar and picturesque cactus, so characteristic of the country, called by the Indians "*petayah*" but more generally known as the "*suaro*" and recognized by botanists as the "*Cereus grandeus.*"

Our next march was to Filibuster camp, eleven miles; thence to Antelope Peak, fifteen Mohawk, twelve; Texas Hill, eleven; Stanwix, seventeen; Burke's, twelve miles. Here we found the reconnoitring party, under Captain Calloway, that had left Fort

Yuma a few days before our arrival there. They had had a brush with the rebels at Picacho, a point about forty-five miles west of Tucson. Lieutenant Barrett, Company A, First Cavalry, California Volunteers, and three men of the same company, had been killed. They had secured three rebel prisoners. The poor devils were under guard beneath some cottonwoods in their camp. They were now on their return to Fort Yuma.

The next morning our command moved out with more alacrity than usual, for we felt that we were now the advance of the "Column," and we would meet the rebels, too. A short march of twelve miles brought us to Oatman Flat. We had come down from the high mesa lands into this valley, and as we passed through near the middle of it, saw upon the right side of the road a small enclosure of rails, on one end of which was inscribed "The Oatman Family."

We had all heard of this tragedy years before, and now we were upon the spot where the terrible massacre had been perpetrated. (*The Oatman Girls* also published by Leonaur). No one of us could look upon this humble monument without awakening a feeling of revenge, and many were the silent pledges given that day that when the opportunity should offer, that at least one shot would be given for these silent victims to Indian treachery. One officer was so affected that he approached Colonel J. R. West, our commanding officer, with the interrogatory: "Colonel, if we should at anytime meet any of these Indians, what course should be pursued towards them?"

"Tell your men when they see a head, hit it if they can!" was the Colonel's quick rejoinder. You may think this to have been rather harsh, but remember we were standing above the remains of the innocent victims of a most terrible tragedy.

A few miles after leaving Oatman's Flat we came to a pile of immense boulders in the centre of a pleasant valley. These were the famous "Pedras Pintados," or painted rocks. A march of fourteen miles brought the command to Kenyon's. The next day, after sixteen miles marching, we arrived at Gila Bend. Here we lay over a day, as our next march was to be to the Maricopa

Wells, forty miles distant, the dreaded Gila Desert.

After marching all night and all of the next day, we approached the Maricopa Wells at about twelve o'clock on the second night. When within a mile of this point, a small reconnoitring party that had been sent ahead of our command, met us and reported that a large force of the rebels had possession of the wells, and from appearances intended to prevent our command from reaching there. This report served to put new life into everybody, notwithstanding that the whole command had now been without sleep for over forty hours, had marched forty miles and was somewhat fatigued.

One company was thrown out as skirmishers, the rest of the command in line of battle. We approached the watering place, and when we arrived there, instead of finding a formidable enemy, we found a half a dozen of our own cavalry that had been scouting ahead of the command. We found the water strongly impregnated with alkali, but it served to assuage our thirst.

A short march of ten miles then brought us to the Casa Blanca, the largest village of the Pimo Indians. Our command remained here for several weeks, until at least a large part of the "Column" had arrived, and large stores of commissaries and forage had been collected. Our Indian scouts and spies brought every few days extravagant reports of the force of rebels at Tucson, and they all agreed that when our troops should reach that point, we would meet with a warm reception, and that rifle-pits, sufficiently manned, extended a long ways on either side of the town.

These Indians were on the best of terms with us, as they had sold large amounts of their produce to our command, for which they had been promptly and abundantly paid a different experience when the rebels were there. They had been employed by our quartermaster's department as herders of our beef cattle, and were paid to their own satisfaction for all services they had rendered, but no inducement that our commander offered them, no amount of pay, could influence any one of them to accompany us towards Tucson, so assured were they that we were to be "wiped out" before we should reach there.

On or about the twelfth day of May, 1862, the advance, constituted as before stated, with B Company, California Cavalry, Captain Emil Fritz, added, left the peaceful and hospitable homes of the Pimos, and arrived at the Sacatone, twelve miles. Here we left the overland mail road, which we had followed since leaving Los Angeles, and keeping up the south bank of the Gila to White's Ranch; thence to the celebrated ruins of the Casa Blanca, so graphically described by Mr. John R. Bartlett in his *Personal Narratives* of the Boundary Commission; thence to Rattlesnake Spring; thence to old Fort Breckenridge, which had been so cowardly deserted the year before by our regular troops; thence to Cañon de Oro.

As we now approached Tucson, everything was infighting trim. A short halt was made near the town, and the cavalry company, in two divisions, approached the place from the north and west. The infantry marched in by the main street from the west, with the field music playing "Yankee Doodle," and instead of being received by shot and shell, we found neither friend nor enemy, only a village without population, if we except some hundreds of dogs and cats.

When we were at the Pimos, Governor Pesquira, of Sonora, Mexico, arrived there from California on his way home; he was allowed to pass our lines; he and his party arrived in Tucson a few days before our command, and found the place nearly deserted. Captain Hunter, with his rebel soldiers, were far on their way to the Rio Grande, and as they had assured the native population— wholly Mexican—that when the "Abs"—meaning the Union troops—arrived they would massacre all the men and abuse all the women, they stood not upon the order of going, but went at once for Sonora.

Governor Pesquira hurried forward, overtaking parties of the fugitives each day, and assuring them of different treatment from the Union soldiers than they had been told by the rebels, induced many to return to their homes, and within a week Tucson was again alive; stores and gambling saloons were numerous, the military had taken possession of the best buildings in the town for quarters, and the stars and stripes again waved over the Capital of the Territory of Arizona.

The advance of the "Column" entered Tucson on the twentieth day of May, 1862. Several Americans, among them Sylvester Mowry, formerly of Rhode Island, returned, and being violent in their sympathies with the rebellion, were arrested. Some were sent out of the Territory, while Mowry was sent to Fort Yuma, where he remained incarcerated a long time. About the fifteenth of June, Captain N. S. Davis was relieved from the command of Company K by Lieutenant Pettis, who remained in command, with a short interval, until its final muster out. Captain Davis was on duty in the quartermaster's department. By the first of July, a large part of the " Column" had arrived at Tucson, a large depot of army stores had been brought from California, and preparations were commenced for the movement again of the advance column.

Several spies and scouts had been sent forward from Tucson, but as they had not returned, matters were rather uncertain. However, in the first week in July, Company E, First California Infantry, Captain Thomas L. Roberts, and Company B, Second California Cavalry, were ordered to proceed to Apache Pass and hold possession of the water at that point. On the twentieth of July the advance column left Tucson, and on the second day arrived at the San Pedro, twenty-five miles. Here a delay of one day was made to put the fording place in good order for the crossing of the "Column."

Information was received here that Captain Roberts' advance into the Apache Pass had been attacked by a large force of the Apaches, under the renowned chief, "Cochise," and after fighting during an entire afternoon had succeeded in driving the Indians, with a loss on our side of several of our men killed and wounded.

Our next march was to Dragoon Springs, eighteen miles; thence to Sulphur Springs, twenty-two miles. The famous Apache Pass was reached by another march of twenty-five miles. Here was found the command of Captain Roberts, with evidences of the struggle of a few days before. On leaving Apache Pass the next day, we were again the advance of the "Column," which position was retained until our arrival on the Rio Grande. The next camping ground was at San Simon, eighteen miles. As we were assured by our guides that no water would be found until we reached *Ojo de Vaca*, or Cow Springs, a distance of sixty-seven miles, it was deemed advisable to leave the overland route at this point, and proceed by another route.

Accordingly, the next morning the command moved south, following up the San Simon Valley, a distance of twelve miles, and camped at the Cienega. Here was found water, the best and most abundant on the whole march. Imagine, if you can, a valley twenty miles in width, on either side a range of mountains; and to the north and south, up and down the valley, a level plain as far as the eye could reach.

A trench three feet wide, by five or six in depth, filled nearly to the top with clear cold water, running with a velocity of at least six miles an hour, the bottom covered with white smooth pebbles. Two miles above this point no water was to be found. As you descended the valley and approached this water, you found at first the ground moist, then water appeared, a mere drop, then a small stream of running water, which increased in volume, until you found a stream as described above. Below this point the water gradually lessened, until, two miles below, this magnificent stream had entirely disappeared.

There was no shade to be had here, except that found under the wagon bodies, still there was no fault found; the fine stream of water that we were enjoying satisfied us for all other discomforts. It was with feelings of regret that we left this point late the next afternoon, with well filled canteens; and the uncertainty of finding water in advance, added to this feeling. We arrived at Leiteresdorffer's Wells soon after sunset, but no water was to be found. The march was continued during the night, and all of the next day, until we arrived at Soldier's Farewell, and no water. The command was strung out a distance of at least five miles; we had been marching thirty hours, with only a canteen each of water, with the thermometer at least 130.

A large number of the men had given out and were scattered in parties of three or four, for a dozen miles in the rear. What was left of the command moved on, and after leaving the wagon road, we arrived in Burro Cañon, sometime after dark, where plenty of water was found, when, after taking in a fill, turned into our blankets, entirely forgetting our hunger in our weariness. Company K marched into Burro Cañon with less than ten men out of eighty, and it was long after daylight the next day before the whole command had arrived. A short march of twelve miles brought us to Ojo de Baca; thence eighteen miles to the Miembres River.

Our next march, twenty-five miles, was to Cooke's Springs, passing through Cooke's Cañon. This location was known by Mexicans as *La Valle del Muerto*, or Valley of Death. It seemed to be rightly named, too, as for nearly two miles were to be seen, on either side, skulls and other portions of human remains who had fallen by Indian assassination. Mounds and crosses were met every few minutes. As we emerged from this *triste* locality, we encountered the remains of wagons and government stores, that had been destroyed the year before by the regular troops, who had deserted Forts Buchanan and Breckenridge, in Arizona. When they had arrived at this point, they were informed of the surrender of the regulars at Fort Fillmore; consequently, without further inquiry, they destroyed all the government property they had in charge, and made their way, on the west side of the Rio Grande, to Fort Craig.

The next march brought us near to Mule Springs, fifteen miles; and on the next afternoon could be discovered, in the distance, the green, winding way of the Rio Grande, with the Sierras de Organos in the background. Camp was made that night on the banks of the Rio Bravo del Norte, near to old Fort Thorn. The next march was down the west bank of the river to the fording place, known as San Diego, which you will find set down on all maps as a town or village, but to my certain knowledge, up to the time mentioned, and for several years afterwards, there was but one house in the vicinity, and that contained but one room and no roof.

As the river was now, the third of August, at its extreme height, caused by the melting of the snow in the upper Rocky Mountains, we experienced some difficulty in getting our wagons and stores across; still all was completed before sundown, and the next day we arrived at Roblado, near the town of Dona Ana. On the fifth of August, after passing through the villages of Dona Ana and Las Cruces, we arrived at the pleasant town of La Mesilla.

Here was to be our resting place. We found a well-built village, with a numerous population, mostly Mexican. The rebels, who had arrived in the Territory, we learned, had, after the treacherous surrender of the regular troops at Fort Fillmore (directly opposite La Mesilla), marched north. They found Fort Craig too strong to be attacked, and, contrary to all military maxims, had continued on, leaving a fortified position in their rear. The desperate battle of Val Verde had taken place on the twenty-first and twenty-second of February, 1862, a short distance above Fort Craig.

And as long as Major Benny Roberts had command of the Federal troops they were successful, but when General E. R. S. Canby came on the field and took command, the rebels soon had turned the tide of the battle in their favour. McRae's battery was taken, and our troops were returning, panic-stricken, across the river, and fleeing towards Fort Craig, about three miles down the river. The rebels then approached Albuquerque, where was stored a large amount of government stores, which were surrendered without a struggle. Thence they proceeded to Santa Fé, where, without opposition, they took possession. There was one other fort to be taken, about one hundred miles northwest—Fort Union.

After some delay at Santa Fé, the rebels, numbering some sixteen hundred, set out for Fort Union. At Apache Pass, or Pigeon's Ranch, they were met by a Colorado regiment, with what regulars and militia could be found, all under command of Colonel John P. Slough (afterwards chief justice of the Territory), and were defeated, their wagons, ammunition, 'and all their stores having been destroyed by a party of Union troops under Captain W. H. Lewis, Fifth United States Infantry, and Captain A. B. Cary, of the Third United States Infantry, who scaled a mountain and got into their rear.

The rebels precipitately retreated from this point, to and down the Rio Grande, having passed La Mesilla a few weeks before our arrival, and left the Territory with about twelve hundred men out of thirty-seven hundred, that they had arrived with.

The different companies of the "Column," as they arrived, were now sent to different points in the department. Our Colonel, James H. Carleton, had been promoted to Brigadier General, and had relieved General E. R. S. Canby, in command of the department of New Mexico. The regular troops were all relieved, except the Fifth Infantry, and sent east, and a protection was now assured to the population, by the California Volunteers. Lieutenant Colonel J. K. West was now promoted to Colonel of the regiment, and in command of the southern district of the department.

Fine quarters were found for the command in the village of La Mesilla, and the district was under martial law. Duty was really pleasant here,—plenty of society, with frequent *bailes*, few drills, and plenty of everything to eat and drink. The white population were nearly all of secession proclivities, one in particular, Samuel L. Jones (better known as the pro-slavery Sheriff Jones, of Kansas), who resided here, was arrested usually about once a week, and incarcerated in the guard-house for treasonable utterances.

After a protracted season of this duty, or up to about the twentieth of November, came the most unpleasant part of the history of Company K. There had been several escapes from the guard-house of persons who had been imprisoned for treasonable utterances, until it seemed that there might exist a disposition among some of the command to be a party to these frequent escapades. This state of affairs existed until one morning an escape was reported to the commanding officer, Colonel West, who immediately ordered the sergeant of the guard, with sentinels numbers one, two, three, four and five, who were on duty at the time, to be placed in the guard-house, in irons.

It so happened that this sergeant and all the sentinels belonged to Company K, and at the morning drill, after guard mount, the company refused to do further duty, or until the irons were taken off of Sergeant Miller. The soldier most aggrieved appeared to be Corporal Charles Smith, or rather he acted as spokesman for the company. The company was immediately ordered into their quarters by Lieutenant Pettis, and put under guard, and the facts reported to the commanding officer. Orders were given for all prisoners to be placed in the guard-house; Company K was ordered to proceed to the *plaza* or parade without arms, when the long roll was beat.

The other two companies of the garrison were soon on the *plaza*, fully equipped. Colonel West now made his appearance, mounted; he then marched Company A, Fifth California Infantry, about five paces in front of and facing Company K, with pieces loaded, and at a "ready." He then called Corporal Smith to the front, and asked him if he still persisted in refusing to do his duty? The corporal respectfully, but firmly, announced that he would do no duty until the irons were removed from Sergeant Miller. Company D, First California Infantry, had been wheeled to the right out of line, and the Corporal was now ordered to place himself about six paces in front of this company.

Upon his again refusing to do duty, Captain Mitchell, of Company D, was ordered to fire upon him. This order was unhesitatingly obeyed; and after the smoke had cleared away, it was seen that the corporal was uninjured. Not so with some others. The position of Company D was such that it was facing the cathedral, which is situated on the west side of the *plaza*; on either side of the cathedral were long straight streets, running from the plaza; the long roll and the other preparations had called all the inhabitants from their residences, and the result of the first volley was to wound two invalid soldiers, together with one Mexican woman and one child, and the cathedral, which was built of adobes, was concealed for a few minutes by its own dust, caused by the minie balls penetrating its front.

The corporal was again questioned by Colonel West, who returned his former answer, and Company D again fired a volley, but the corporal remained untouched. After another questioning by the colonel, Company D was once more ordered to fire, when, between the commands "aim," "fire," Colonel West rode up behind the company with uplifted sabre, and gave the command to " lower those rifles," when the command was given by the captain to "fire." At this discharge, the corporal fell to the ground, a minie ball having passed directly through him, having entered his right breast. He was immediately placed upon a stretcher, and expired on his way to the hospital.

The rest of the company was now questioned by Colonel West, and each man asserted his willingness to do his duty, when the command was dismissed to their quarters, and Company K immediately assumed their arms and accoutrements and appeared upon the *plaza* for drill. This was the only evidence of insubordination ever shown in the " Column," and the prompt manner in which this one was met and punished, precluded any danger of another exhibition of this character.

A few days after these occurrences, some of our spies and scouts brought in the intelligence that another large party of rebels had left San Antonio, Texas, for New Mexico. Accordingly, Companies K and D were ordered to San Elizario, Texas, a town about twenty-five miles below El Paso, Mexico, and the last point of civilization towards San Antonio, on outpost duty. After remaining here about six weeks, and no rebels appearing, Company K was ordered to Fort Craig. A march of twenty-five miles brought us to Franklin or Fort Bliss, directly opposite El Paso; thence two marches, aggregating fifty miles, found us in our old quarters at La Mesilla, where the company was ordered to remain until the adjournment of a general court-martial which was then in session at that post.

A week later, and Company K commenced its march for Fort

Craig. A short march brought us again to Dona Ana. Three miles from that village brought us to the commencement of the much dreaded *Jornada del Muerto* (Journey of Death). The *Jornada* is a large desert, well supplied with fine *gramma* grass in some portions, but absolutely destitute of water or shade for seventy-five miles. Why it ever received its title, I never distinctly learned, but suppose it was on account of the very numerous massacres committed on it by the Apache Indians.

On the east, in the far distance, are the Sierras Blancos, and is fringed on the west by the Sierra Caballo and Sierra de Frey Cristobal. From these heights, on either side, the Indians are enabled to distinctly perceive any party of travellers coming over the wide and unsheltered expanse of the *Jornada del Muerto*. When any such parties are seen, they come sweeping down upon the unsuspecting immigrant in more than usual numbers, and if successful, as they generally are, in their attack, invariably destroy all of the party, for there is no possible chance of escape; and the Apaches never take any prisoners but women and young children, and they become captives for life.

The first camp was a dry one, and as the command was accompanied by a tank of water, drawn by six mules, thus being prepared by a plentiful supply of water, I concluded to cross this desert at my leisure. The next forenoon we passed by the celebrated "Point of Rocks," the company being deployed as skirmishers, with the hope of finding Indians hiding between the huge boulders of which it was composed, but without results. Late in the afternoon we arrived at the Aleman, so called from the fact that a whole German immigrant family had been massacred at this point some years before by the Indians.

The next night another dry camp, having passed during the day the *Laguna del Muerto*, where water is found in some seasons. While some three miles on our left was the *Ojo del Muerto*, a point where Fort McRae was established in 1863 by Captain Henry A. Greene, commanding Company G, First California Infantry, now a resident of this city, (Providence, R. I.) The next day's march brought us to the little village of El Paraje del Fra

Cristobal. Near the spot on which the camp was made, was the peaceful flowing and muddy Rio Grande. A short march of five miles brought us to our destination—Fort Craig. Our arrival was in January, 1863.

The company remained at this post during the year 1863, monotony of garrison life being relieved by furnishing escorts to wagon trains bound north and south, and an occasional scout after Indians. In July of that year, Assistant Surgeon Watson, who had been commissioned at Sacramento, California, more than a year before, and had been ordered to report to the headquarters of his regiment at Fort Craig, arrived at Fort McRae, without accident. On leaving that post, Captain Greene had furnished him with one government wagon and an escort of five or six men of his company. They set out with joyful anticipation; the doctor was delighted to know that after a year's travel, he would soon be at his new home, and be doing duty with his own regiment, which he had never seen.

The wagon, with its occupants, soon emerged from the *cañon* of the *Ojo del Muerto*, and came out on the hard, smooth, natural road of the *Jornada*. About the middle of the afternoon, they were proceeding leisurely along; twelve miles in advance could be plainly seen the buildings of Fort Craig, with "Old Glory " on the flag-staff. The driver of the team, Johnson, a soldier of Greene's company, sat on his near wheel-mule chatting pleasantly with the doctor, who occupied the front of the wagon, with his feet hanging down on the whiffle-trees; the escort were all in the wagon, lying on their blankets, with their arms and equipments beneath them.

Within five miles of them there was not a rock, tree, shrub, or bush, as large as a man's head—they felt a perfect security. Another moment, how changed! There arose from the sand of the desert, where they had buried themselves, some ten or twelve Apaches, within twenty feet of the moving wagon, and poured a volley of arrows into the doomed party, and closing in immediately, a part attacked the occupants of the wagon, while the rest disengaged the mules, and mounting their backs started for the mountains on the west, towards the river, and before the soldiers were out of the wagon were out of reach of their fire.

Doctor Watson was shot with two arrows, one in his right arm, and the other on the inside of his right thigh, severing the femoral artery. He breathed his last in a few minutes; the driver was shot through the heart, and one or two of the escorts were slightly wounded. News of this affair reached the post before sunset, and in twenty minutes Company K was on its way down the west side of the river to intercept, if possible, these murderers. The company was kept in the field for thirty days, without other result than to find a hot trail of eighty-two Navajoes, who were on their way to their own country, with some eight thousand head of sheep and other stock that they had stolen in the upper counties of New Mexico.

As the company were dismounted, it was impossible to take up the trail. The commander of the company, however, with five cavalrymen and two Mexican scouts, followed and overtook the Indians after a run of twenty-five miles, but accomplished nothing except exchanging some twenty or twenty-five shots on either side, as our animals were completely "blown," and eighty-two to eight was an unpleasant disparity of numbers. The lieutenant and his men arrived back at the river the next morning, having been in the saddle nearly twenty-four hours. The result of the short skirmish was that one of the cavalrymen's horses was shot through the breast, and one Navajo was sent to his happy hunting-grounds and one was wounded.

January, 1864, Company K was ordered to Los Pinos, about one hundred miles further up the Rio Grande, and about twenty miles south of Albuquerque; marching through the towns of Socoreo, La Limitar, across the sand hills at the foot of the *Sierra de los Ladrones*, or Thieves Mountains; crossing the Rio Puerco, near its affluence with the Rio Grande; thence to Sabinal, La Belen, and Los Lunes. They remained here until the first of February, when Colonel Kit Carson arrived there from the Navajo country, with some two hundred and fifty-three Navajo Indians, whom he had taken prisoners in his operations against that nation.

Orders were received from department headquarters for Company K to proceed with these Indians to the Bosque Redonde, some two hundred and fifty miles down on the Pecos River. Accordingly, after formally receiving these prisoners and receipting therefore the command moved out, and on the second night arrived at Carnwell Cañon; thence to San Antonio, San Antoinette, Los Placeres and Gallisteo. Thus far the command had moved across the country, but on the day of leaving Gallisteo, the company struck the military road leading from Fort Union to Santa Fé, near the old Peces ruins.

The command moved along this road to the village of Tecolote; from here they proceeded down the Pecos River, and arrived at Fort Sumner after eighteen days' marching. Fort Sumner was a new post, established for the purpose of a reservation for Indians, both Navajo and Apache, that should be taken prisoners by the troops, and Colonel Carson was on a campaign against the Navajos, in which he was successful, as there were finally some eight thousand of these Indians captured and placed on this reservation. Those brought in by Company K were the first large body that had arrived. I will say here, in parenthesis, that this is the only way to treat the Indian question; for this Indian nation (the Navajoes), after receiving a severe drubbing by Carson, and all had surrendered, were finally allowed to return to their own country, since which time they have continued on the best of terms with our people. This has always been the experience on the frontiers—one effective campaign is better than all the treaties that were ever consummated.

Fort Sumner was at this time in command of Major Henry D. Wallen, United States Seventh Infantry, than whom there was no more excellent gentleman in the service of the government. His administration was marked by a sincere desire to do justice to all under him, a feature that was sadly deficient in too many officers of the time that is spoken of. He was a perfect example of sobriety, and his case certainly was a commendation of the excellence of education of the academy at West Point, of which

84

he was an honoured graduate.

Company K had been at Fort Sumner but a few days when it was ordered to report to the commanding officer at Fort Union, necessitating a march of one hundred and twenty-five miles. The command arrived at Fort Union on the eighteenth day of March, 1864, and remained there, doing camp duty, during the months of April, May and June. In July, the company proceeded, with a company of New Mexican cavalry, towards the east, by the route known as the Cummarron route, passing on our way, Burgwin's Spring, named after the gallant Captain Burgwin, First Regiment United States Dragoons, who fell while leading the attack upon the insurgents at Taos, 1847, and the Wagon Mound, a high landmark (so called from its shape).

From this point to the "Point of Rocks," forty miles, is the track of a bloody, brave and disastrous fight made by eight passengers in the stage against a band of sixty Apaches. They fought every inch of the long, dread struggle. Killed one by one, and dropped on the road, two survivors maintained their defence a long time, and when the sole contestant was left, his last dying effort was to strew the contents of his powder-horn in the sand, and stir it in with his foot, so that the Indians could not use it. Wilson's Creek, some miles further on, is named after a Mr. Wilson, a merchant of Santa Fé, who was overtaken here by the Indians, and, with his wife and child—for he was alone with them—butchered with the usual savage outrage and cruelty.

The command returned to Fort Union in September, in which month the First Infantry, California Volunteers, was mustered out of service, their term of three years having expired, with the exception of Company K, it being recollected that they were enlisted at San Francisco some time after the other companies had been formed. However, the members of that company began, in October, to be dropped out, and when orders arrived at Fort Union for the formation of the Commanche expedition, under Colonel Kit Carson, there remained of the First Infantry Regiment, California Volunteers, one officer (Lieutenant Pettis) and twenty-six enlisted men of Company K.

This company accompanied Carson's expedition with two mountain howitzers, mounted on prairie carriages, and rendezvoused at Fort Bascom, on the Canadian river, near the line of Texas. This expedition consisted as follows: Colonel Christopher Carson, First New Mexico Cavalry, commanding; Colonel Francisco P. Abreú, First New Mexico Infantry; Major William McCleave, First California Cavalry; Captain Emil Fritz, Company B, First California Cavalry, one officer and forty enlisted men; Lieutenant Sullivan Heath, Company K, First California Cavalry, one officer and forty men; Captain Meriam, Company M, First California Cavalry, one officer and thirty-four men; Lieutenant George H. Pettis, Company K, First California Infantry, one officer and twenty-six men; Captain Charles Deus, Company M, First New Mexico Cavalry, two officers and seventy men; Captain Joseph Berney, Company D, First New Mexico Cavalry, two officers and thirty-six men; Company A, First California Veteran Infantry, seventy-five men; Assistant Surgeon George S. Courtright, United States Volunteers, and an officer whose name escapes me, as Assistant Quartermaster and Commissary,—numbering in all, fourteen officers and three hundred and twenty-one enlisted men.

In addition to the command, Colonel Carson had induced seventy-two friendly Indians (Utes and Apaches) , and as big scoundrels as there were on the frontiers, by promising them all the plunder that they might acquire, to join the expedition.

On the sixth of November, the command left Fort Bascom, and proceeded down on the north bank of the Canadian, hoping to find the Commanche and Kiowa Indians (who had been committing their atrocities during the whole of 1864) in their winter quarters. The Indians with our command, on every night, after making camp, being now on the war-path, indulged in the accustomed war dance, which, although new to most of us, became almost intolerable, it being kept up each night until nearly daybreak; and until we became accustomed to their groans and howlings, incident to the dance, it was impossible to sleep. Each morning of our march, two of our Indians would be sent ahead several hours before we started, who would return to camp at night and report.

We had been on our march day after day without particular incident until our arrival at Mule Creek, when our scouts brought in the intelligence that they had seen signs of a large body of Indians that had moved that day, and that they could be overtaken without much effort . Immediately after supper, all of the cavalry, with Company K, moved out of camp in light marching order, leaving the infantry, under command of Colonel Abreú, to protect the wagon train and proceed on our trail on the morrow. Colonel Carson and command marched all night, except a short halt just before dawn, and struck an outpost of the enemy on the opposite side of the river, at about sunrise, who being mounted retreated, followed by our Indians and two companies of our cavalry.

The rest of the command moved down on the north side of the river, and a few miles below the cavalry struck a Kiowa *rancheria* of one hundred and seventy-six lodges, the Indians retreating down the river on their approach. Company K, escorted by Lieutenant Heath's command, and accompanied by Colonel Carson, could not advance with the rapidity of the cavalry, as the cannoneers were dismounted, and the wheels tracking very narrow, caused the utmost attention to prevent their being overturned. The Indians from the Kiowa encampment retreated until they were reinforced by a large force of Commanches from a Commanche *rancheria* of five hundred lodges, a short distance below the "Adobe Walls," a location well known by all frontiersmen.

The cavalry made a stand here, and were engaged in skirmishing with the enemy, when Company K came on the field with the two mountain howitzers. An order from Colonel Carson to Lieutenant Pettis to "fling a few shell over thar!" indicating with his hand a large body of Indians who appeared to be about to charge into our forces, that officer immediately ordered "Battery halt! action right, load with shell—load!" Before the fourth discharge of the howitzers, the Indians had retreated out of range, and it was supposed that there would be no more fighting; but we counted without our host, for our animals had scarcely been watered when the enemy returned to the conflict. The horses of the cavalry were again placed in the "Adobe Walls," which were elevated enough to protect them from the rifle balls of the enemy, and the fight was soon at its height.

About the middle of the afternoon, Carson concluded to return to the Kiowa village that we had passed through in the morning, contrary to the wishes of his officers, who were anxious to advance to the Commanche village, which was less than a mile in our front. The return column consisted of the cavalry horses, the number four of each set of fours leading the other three horses, with the howitzers in the rear, the dismounted cavalry acting as skirmishers on the front, rear and either flank. The firing was continued from each side until the village was reached, when our troops proceeded to destroy it, which was effectually done before dark.

A further march of about four miles, and the wagon train was reached, the safety of which had been the subject of much anxiety during the day. The gun carriages and ammunition carts of Company K were packed with the wounded on their return from the Kiowa village. A rest was had the next day, which was sadly needed, as the whole command had been marching and fighting about twenty-seven hours, on a few broken hard tack and a slice of salt pork each.

The second day after the fight, Carson concluded to return to Fort Bascom, which post was reached in twenty-one days. Here the command remained until orders were received from General Carleton, commanding the department, and Company K was ordered to Fort Union, as the term of service of nearly all the men had expired.

By the first of February, 1865, all the enlisted men of the company had been mustered out of service, and Lieutenant Pettis, the last man of his regiment, was ordered to report to the mustering officer at Santa Fé, with all the records of his company; and on the fifteenth of February, he was mustered out of service, and Company K, First Infantry, California Volunteers, had ceased to exist, having marched on foot during its term of service four thousand two hundred and forty-five miles.

Kit Carson's Fight With the Comanche and Kiowa Indians

George H. Pettis

BRIGADIER GENERAL CHRISTOPHER C.
CARSON, UNITED STATES VOLUNTEERS,
"KIT CARSON,"

Taken in Boston, Mass. about March
25, 1868, during a visit to Washington
and Eastern Cities with a band of Ute
Indians.

Contents

Kit Carson's Fight With the Comanche and Kiowa Indians

November 1864

The summer of 1864 will long be remembered by our frontiersmen as a season when the Comanche, the Kiowa, the Arapahoe, the Cheyenne, and the Plain Apache held high carnival on our western plains. From the early spring of that year, when the hardy Indian pony could subsist on the growing grass of the prairies, until late in the fall, they committed their depredations, and there was not a week of that whole season, but that some outrage was committed by them. They seemed to have conceived the idea that the white man could be exterminated, and by concerted action, and by striking at different points, to have fondly hoped that they could once more roam and hunt at their pleasure, free and unmolested by the white man's civilization.

The determined operations of the western Indians and their concerted action at this time, has led some to believe that it was a part of the programme of, and that they had been incited to this by, the leaders of the rebellion. It seems plausible, too, for when the grand old Army of the Potomac was fighting the battles of the Wilderness, of Spottsylvania, of North Anna, of Cold Harbor, and Petersburg, and the Weldon Railroad, Ream's Station, Peeble's Farm, and Boydtown Road; and Sheridan had ridden his "twenty miles from Winchester town" and had driven Early out of the Shenandoah Valley; and Sherman was fighting the battles that led to the capture of Atlanta, the Indians were spreading havoc and destruction in all directions.

No trains crossed the plains that season without being attacked, and none but those with strong military escorts escaped capture and destruction. Houses and barns on the frontier were fired, stock of all kinds was nowhere secure, large and small parties were attacked, men, women, and children murdered. In fact, the year 1864 will be sadly remembered as long as the present generation of frontiersmen lives. The commanders of the different military departments bordering on this territory, had, with the few men at their command, sent out during the summer several expeditions, as escorts to trains, but they had accomplished no more than to accord safety to their different charges, as the mode of Indian warfare is to only give battle when they have all of the advantages.[1]

In the month of October, 1864, Brigadier General James H. Carleton, United States Volunteers then commanding the Department of New Mexico, believing that the Commanches and Kiowas might be found, on the south side of the Canadian River, in winter quarters, issued a general order, directing an expedition against these Indians.

The command was ordered to consist as follows: Colonel Christopher Carson, (familiarly known as "Kit Carson,") First New Mexico Cavalry, commanding; Colonel Francisco P. Abreú, First New Mexico Infantry; Major William McCleave, First California Cavalry; Captain Emil Fritz, Company B, First California Cavalry, one officer and forty enlisted men; Lieutenant Sullivan Heath, Company K, First California Cavalry, one officer and forty men; Captain Merriam, Company M, First California Cavalry, one officer and thirty-four men; Lieutenant George H. Pettis, Company K, First California Infantry, one officer and twenty-six men, with two twelve pounder mountain howitzers mounted on prairie carriages; Captain Charles Deus, Company M., First New Mexico Cavalry, two officers and sev-

1. At the reading of this paper, before the Soldiers and Sailors Historical Society, February 14th, 1877, a gentleman who had visited the Indian Territory immediately at the close of the War, of the Rebellion, assured me that the supposition that the confederate authorities of the late war had incited the Indians to commit their atrocities in 1864, was founded on face, he having been so informed by several of the principal chiefs as that time.—G. H. P

enty men; Captain Joseph Berney, Company D, First New Mexico Cavalry, two officers and thirty-six men; Company A, First California Veteran Infantry, seventy-five men; Assistant Surgeon George S. Courtright, United States Volunteers, and an officer, whose name has escaped me, as Assistant Quartermaster and Commissary,—numbering, in all, fourteen officers and three hundred and twenty-one enlisted men.

Of this number, Company A, 1st California Infantry (Veteran,) one officer and seventy-five men, remained with the wagon train, and took no part in the fight, which left thirteen officers and two hundred and forty-six men that participated with Carson.

In addition to the command, Colonel Carson had induced seventy-two friendly Indians (Utes and Apaches,) by promising them all the plunder that they might acquire, to join the expedition. These Utes and Apaches are known among frontiersmen as "Mountain Indians," in contradistinction to the "Plain Indians," and make their homes in the Rocky Mountains, to the north and west of the Mexican town of Don Fernando de Taos. As Carson had been their agent at one time, and they knowing him well, he had little difficulty in inducing them to join him on an expedition against their old enemies.

The troops mentioned above were stationed at different posts in the Territory of New Mexico, and they were ordered to rendezvous at Fort Bascom, a frontier post on the Canadian River near the boundary line of Texas, on the fourth of November. The quartermaster had received his supplies in a train of twenty-seven wagons and an ambulance, and the morning of the sixth of November found the command ready to stretch out, the horses having all been well shod, and after some difficulty in crossing the Canadian River, to the north side, the expedition was well on the war path before noon, and went into camp that night at the mouth of Ute Creek, near the boundary line of New Mexico and Texas.

From this time the command moved on from day to day, with only such incidents as usually accompany such expeditions, except that it was a new country to most of us, as our campaigning had never extended to the plains before this time, we heretofore having operated against the Navajoe and Apache Indians in the immediate vicinity of the Rio Grande, extending our scouting at times into the eastern and northern parts of Arizona. On our third or fourth day out from Fort Bascom, we passed the vicinity where Kit Carson had, fifteen or twenty years before this time, pursued a marauding band of Comanches, who had attacked a wagon train near Fort Union in New Mexico; all the men of the train had been killed, including a Mr. White, an American, whose wife and child had been taken prisoners.

Carson, who was in that vicinity at the time, organized a party and proceeded on the trail, and after several days, had come up to them at this point. They being well into their own country had not anticipated being pursued so far. The party of whites attacked them at early dawn, drove them from their camp, and found only the reeking bodies of Mrs. White and her child, still warm, with their life's blood slowly ebbing away, the Indians having, as is usual with them, at the first sound of the attack, perforated the bodies of their prisoners with spears and arrows. Carson explained to us how their attack was made, the position of the Indian camp, where the bodies were found, etc. in his usual graphic manner.

The Indians with our command, on every night after making camp, being now on the war path, indulged in their war dance, which, although new to most of us, became almost intolerable, it being kept up each night until nearly daybreak, and until we became accustomed to their groans and howlings incident to the dance, it was impossible to sleep. Each morning of our march, two of our Indians would be sent ahead several hours before we started, who would return to camp at night and report. On the fifteenth we arrived and made camp at the Cañada de los Ruedes, or Wheel Gulch, so called from the fact that years before, when New Mexico was a state of Old Mexico, the Mexican trains on their way to the States for goods, with their *carretas*, or ox carts, usually remained over here for repairs, and as the cottonwood trees were larger than at any other point on their route, they could obtain such a supply of new wheels as their necessities required—hence the name of "*Cañada de los Ruedes.*"

We had up to this time followed on the old Mexican road from New Mexico, the first party that had passed over it for years, as it had been long in disuse, the usual route being by way of the Cimarron and Arkansas Rivers, several hundred miles farther north. Near this point, the old wagon road left the valley of the Canadian, and turned abruptly to the north, while we, keeping to the right, found an old, unused Indian trail, which kept in the direction of the Canadian. We had been fortunate in having good weather, for that season of the year, and something very unusual in scouting on the frontier, we had been successful in finding plenty of water, both for the men and for our animals.

On the afternoon of November twenty-fourth, after a short march of eighteen miles, we made camp at Mule Spring, having marched through the State of Texas and arrived in the western part of the Indian Territory. Up to this time no indications of hostile Indians had been observed, although Carson made good use of his many years of frontier experience, by keeping his Indian scouts well out on either flank. We had arrived at Mule Spring early in the afternoon; had performed our usual camp duties, and as the sun was about setting, many of us being at supper, we were surprised to see our Indians, who were lying around the camp, some gambling, some sleeping, and others waiting for something to eat from the soldiers' mess, spring to their feet, as if one man, and gaze intently to the eastward, talking in their own language quite excitedly.

Upon questioning Colonel Carson, why this tumult among our Indians, he informed us that the two scouts that he had dispatched that morning, had found the Comanches, and were now returning to report the particulars. Although the returning scouts were at least two miles distant, and, mounted on their ponies, were hardly discernible, yet the quick, sharp eye of our Indians made them out without difficulty. I must confess that I failed to see them, until an Indian pointed out to me, away off on the hill side, two mere specks moving towards our camp. And what was more remarkable, they had, by a single shout, in that rarefied, electrical atmosphere, conveyed the intelligence that they had found the enemy, and that work was to be done.

But a short time elapsed before the two scouts arrived, and rode leisurely through cramp, without answering any questions or giving any information, until they had found the colonel, when they reported that they had, about ten miles in advance, found, indications that a large body of Indians had moved that morning, with a very large herd of horses and cattle, and that we would have no difficulty in finding all the Indians that we desired. Carson immediately ordered all the cavalry, and the section of mountain howitzers, to be ready to move without delay. The Infantry, Company A, First California Infantry, under command of Colonel Abreú, was ordered to remain as escort to the wagon train, which was to stay in camp that night, and on the morrow was to move on and follow the trail of the command, until they overtook it.

Just before dark, Carson, with his command, moved out of camp, in light marching order, with strict orders that, during the night march, there should be no talking or smoking. Before twelve we had descended again into the valley of the Canadian, which we had left four days before, and had also found in the dark, the deep-worn, fresh trail of the hostile Indians. At this time, we believed that we were in the immediate vicinity of the enemy, and as nothing of their position was known to us, it was deemed prudent to remain where we were, and move on again just before daylight. This halt was very tedious.

As I said before, no talking was allowed, (the few orders that were necessary, were given in a whisper,) lighting of pipes and smoking was prohibited; each officer and soldier upon halting, only dismounted, and remained holding his horse by the bridle rein until morning; and to add to our discomforts a heavy frost fell during the night.

As the first grey streaks of dawn appeared in the eastern skies, we mounted our horses, and proceeded on our new-found trail. Our order of march was, first on the right, Colonel Carson in company with the Utes and Apaches, who generally kept no regular order; next came about one-half of the cavalry force;

Inscription on rock in Keams Cañon, Arizona, by the soldiers of the First Regiment, New Mexico Volunteers Infantry, August 13, 1862, during an expedition against the Navajos, under command of General Christopher C. Carson, United States Volunteers, "Kit Carson."

then the section of mountain howitzers; the balance of the cavalry bringing up the rear. We had been moving but a few minutes, when I was informed that Carson wished to see me at the head of the column. I urged my horse forward as quietly as I could, and reported to him.

As I did so, I remarked the funny appearance of his Indians, all of whom were mounted in their peculiar manner, with their knees drawn up nearly at right angles, and being cold, they were each of them enveloped in their buffalo robes, standing high above their heads, and fastened by a belt at their waist. Such a sight was ludicrous in the extreme. Carson commenced to say to me, in his own quaint way: "I had a dream the night before, of being engaged with a large number of Indians; your cannons were firing,"—at this point of his recital, we heard a voice in Spanish, on the opposite side of the river, cry out "*Bene-acá*," "*Bene-acá*,"—"Come here," "Come here." We knew that we had found a picket of the enemy. Carson hastily ordered Major Mc-Cleave, and B Company First California Cavalry, with one of the New Mexico detachments, to cross the river, as it was easily forded.

Our Indians, who had been riding leisurely along, at the first cry charged into a clump of chaparral which was nearby, and in a moment, as it seemed, came riding out again, completely divested of buffalo robes and all their clothing, with their bodies covered with war paint, and war feathers in abundance, and giving a war-whoop they dashed wildly into the river towards the enemy. I was wondering at the wonderful transformation of our Indians, entirely forgetful of the enemy, when Carson gave orders for us to move down on our side of the river, he being satisfied that the village would be found within a short distance.

A few shots were fired on the opposite side of the river, and we soon saw by the early morning light, the enemy's picket, consisting of three mounted Indians, rushing madly on, followed by the detachments that had been sent over. We had proceeded but a short distance, when Carson ordered our force to move on more rapidly, and strike the Indian village before they should become fully, alarmed, while he himself, with Lieutenant

Heath's detachment, remained as escort to the battery, the carriages of which were so small that the cannoneers could not be mounted, consequently they could not move as fast as the rest of the command, which was composed entirely of cavalry, it being remembered that the infantry had remained behind the night before at Mule Creek, as escort to the wagon train.

It was not long before the cavalry had disappeared from our sight, as we were now in the middle of the rich valley of the Canadian River, which was here about two miles in width, with occasional clumps of cottonwood trees, and covered with tall dry grass, in many places high above our heads when mounted on our horses. In fact, I remember that several times during that morning, when riding with Colonel Carson, and keeping up a conversation, we could not see each other, the tall dry grass intervening. This tall grass and an occasional clump of drift-wood, which had been formed by previous freshets of the river, made hard work for us to get along with the mountain howitzers.

The carriages having low wheels, and tracking very narrow, the most constant care and attention would not prevent their occasional capsizing and consequent delay in righting up again. We were an hour probably in getting through this wilderness, and getting out on to clear, hard, unobstructed earth again, by which time we could hear, far in advance, rifle shots thick and fast. The quick, sharp command, "Trot—MARCH," would be given to the battery, which would move out at a trot for a few hundred yards, when the dismounted cannoneers would soon be left stringing out a long way to the rear; "Walk—MARCH," would be resumed, so as to allow the men to regain their places, and after allowing them a short time to regain their breath, the same movements would be again and again performed.

At about nine o'clock, the firing in our advance, which was becoming more rapid, seemed to be moving forward faster than we were, or rather it seemed that every minute, the distance between ourselves and the. firing parties was becoming wider, yet we were all the time advancing. We now came upon a large number of cattle, belonging to the Kiowas, that were quietly browsing on the plain, entirely oblivious of war's destruction in their midst. Shortly after, we saw a number of our Indians, each having his own separate herd of from twenty to fifty of the enemy's ponies, and on getting them a short distance away from each other, each would single out and of the best of his respective herd, dismount, and placing his riding outfit upon his new steed, would leave his own worn out pony to mark his individual property, expecting that the fight would be over in a few minutes, when they were to return, and according to their terms of contract for the campaign, each would have his own separate herd of horses, which he had collected, and which was marked by the horse left by him.

A long low hill, stretching from the foothills across the valley of the Canadian to the river, which was here forced to the opposite side of the valley, next met our view, over the top of which could be seen a larger number of what I supposed to be Sibley tents from their shape and whiteness, and I so expressed my opinion to Colonel Carson, who informed me that they were Indian lodges made of buffalo hide whitened by a process practiced by all the Indians on the plains. I do not remember of having been deceived at any time as I was by these lodges; positive I was that they were Sibley tents, and this opinion was also that of my enlisted men buffalo lodges are not used by the mountain Indians—but in the next minute we passed through the centre of this village, when we were fully satisfied.

Our advance, which was a long way ahead of us. had surprised the Kiowas in their lodges which formed this village. The bucks or males had seized their weapons and ammunition and retreated down the river followed by our men, the women and children, before we came up, had also deserted the village and were hidden in the foothills on our left, which we knew nothing of, unfortunately, as they had an American woman and two children with them, being the widow and children of a sergeant of Colorado volunteers who had been killed in the early part of the season in western Kansas.

The firing continued in our front. Carson said to me that we should proceed, and if the fight was not over when we arrived it would soon be, when we would all return and burn the lodges. At the same time, he threw his heavy military overcoat on a bush alongside the road, and advised me to do the same, as we should return in a few minutes and get them again. I did not do it, however. Some of my men wished to take their overcoats and blankets from the guns and leave them, but I would not allow them to do so, and for once, my judgement was better than Carson's for he never saw that coat of his again, while my own and those of my men did good service afterwards.

But as we pushed on, the firing seemed no nearer, until after we had made about four miles from the village, when we saw our men, dismounted and deployed as skirmishers, with their horses corralled in an old, deserted, *adobe* building, known by all frontiersmen as the Adobe Walls. When we were within about a thousand yards of this point, Carson, with Lieutenant Heath and his detachment, put spurs to their horses and charged forward to join in the fray. My men seemed to get new life, and forgot all their fatigues, at the prospect of going into action, and but a few minutes elapsed before we came into the centre of the field at a gallop, and touching my cap to Carson, I received from him the following order: "Pettis, throw a few shell into that crowd over thar."

The next moment, "Battery, halt! action right,—load with shell—LOAD!" was ordered.

It was now near ten o'clock in the morning, the sky was not obscured by a single cloud, and the sun was shining in all its brightness. Within a hundred yards of the corralled horses in the Adobe Walls, was a small symmetrical conical hill of twenty-five or thirty feet elevation, while in all directions extended a level plain. Carson, McCleave, and a few other officers, occupied the summit, when the battery arrived and took position nearly on the top. Our cavalry was dismounted and deployed as skirmishers in advance, lying in tall grass, and firing an occasional shot at the enemy. Our Indians, mounted and covered with paint and feathers, were charging backwards and forwards and shouting their war cry, and in their front were about two hundred Comanches and Kiowas, equipped as they themselves were, charging in the same manner, with their bodies thrown over the sides of their horses, at a full run, and shooting occasionally under their horses twelve or fourteen hundred, with a dozen or more chiefs riding up and down their line haranguing them, seemed to be preparing for a desperate charge on our forces. Surgeon Courtright had prepared a corner of the Adobe Walls for a hospital, and was busy, with his assistants, in attending to the wants of half a dozen or more wounded. Fortunately, the Adobe Walls were high enough to protect all our horses from the enemy's rifles, and afford ample protection to our wounded. Within a mile of us, beyond the enemy in full and complete view, was a Comanche village of over five hundred lodges, which, with the village that we had captured, made about seven hundred lodges, which allowing two fighting Indians to a lodge, which is the rule on the frontier, would give us fourteen hundred warriors in the field before us.

This was the prospect when the battery came on the ground. A finer sight I never saw before, and probably shall never see again. The Indians seemed to be astonished when the pieces came up at a gallop and were being unlimbered. The pieces were loaded in a few seconds after the order was given, and were sighted by the gunners, when the command "Number one—FIRE!" was given, followed quickly by "Number two—FIRE!" At the first discharge, everyone of the enemy, those that were charging backwards and forwards on their horses but a moment before as well as those that were standing in line, rose high in their stirrups and gazed, for a single moment, with astonishment, then guiding their horses' heads away from us, and giving one concerted, prolonged yell, they started in a dead run for their village.

In fact when the fourth shot was fired there was not a single enemy within the extreme range of the howitzers. Colonel Carson now assured us that the fighting was over, and that the enemy would not make another stand, and gave orders that after a short halt, to allow the men to eat something and to water our horses, as neither man nor beast had received any nourishment since supper time the day before, we were to proceed and capture the Comanche village before us. Accordingly the

106

skirmishers were called in, the cavalry horses were unsaddled, the artillery horses unhitched from the pieces, and all taken a hundred yards or more in our rear, to as fine a running brook of clear cold water as I ever saw on the frontiers.

The horses were allowed to drink their fill, and then each one was picketed with a long lariat, or rope, to eat high, rich, uncropped grass. This accomplished, the officers and men proceeded to fish from the inmost recesses of their haversacks, such pieces of raw bacon and broken hard-bread as they had been fortunate enough to capture the night before on leaving the wagons. Each one had something to relate about the day's conflict, and each one was anxious to know what was to be the result of the day's operations.

Less than half an hour had elapsed, and Carson had not, as yet, given the order to saddle up, when the enemy were returning and seemed to be anxious to renew the conflict. Presently the order came to saddle up, the artillery horses were hitched in again, the cavalry horses returned to the inside of the Adobe Walls, the sharp, quick whiz of the Indians' rifle balls was again heard, the cavalrymen were deployed as before, and the fight was going on again in earnest.

During this fight, which lasted all the afternoon, the howitzers were fired but a few times, as the enemy were shrewd enough to know that their policy was to act singly and avoid getting into masses, although the detachments were kept on the field in the most exposed situations. At one of the discharges, the shell passed directly through the body of a horse on which was a Comanche riding at a full run, and went some two or three hundred yards further on before it exploded.

The horse, on being struck, went head-foremost to earth, throwing his rider hands and feet sprawling in all directions, and as he struck the earth, apparently senseless, two other Indians who were nearby, proceeded to him, one on each side, and throwing themselves over on the sides of their horses, seized each an arm and dragged him from the field between them, amid a shower of rifle balls from our skirmishers. This act of the Indians in removing their dead and helpless wounded from the field is always done, and more than a score of times were we eye-witnesses to this feat during the afternoon. General G. A. Custer, in his *Life on the Plains*," (also published by Leonaur as *My Life on the Plains or Personal Experiences With Indians*), says of this Indian custom, in giving an account of an Indian fight near Fort Wallace, in 1867;

"Those of the savages who were shot from their saddles were scarcely permitted to fall to the ground, before a score or more of their comrades dashed to their rescue, and bore their bodies beyond the possible reach of our men. This is in accordance with the Indian custom in battle. They will risk the lives of a dozen of their best warriors to prevent the body of any one of their number from falling into the white man's possession. The reason for this is the belief, which generally prevails among all the tribes, that if a warrior loses his scalp, he forfeits his hope of ever reaching the happy hunting ground."

But to return again to my story: Quite a number of the enemy acted as skirmishers, being dismounted and hid in the tall grass in our front, and made it hot for most of us by their excellent markmanship, while quite the larger part of them, mounted and covered with their war dresses, charged continually across our front, from right to left and *vice versa*, about two hundred yards from our line of skirmishers, yelling like demons, and firing from under the necks of their horses at intervals. About two hundred yards in rear of their line, all through the fighting at the Abobe Walls, was stationed one of the enemy who had a cavalry bugle, and during the entire day he would blow the opposite call that was used by the officer in our line of skirmishers.

For instance, when our bugles sounded the "advance," he would blow "retreat"; and when ours sounded the "retreat," he would follow with the "advance"; ours would signal "halt;" he would follow suit. So he 'kept it up all the day, blowing as shrill and clearly as our very best buglers. Carson insisted that it was a white man, but I have never received any information to corroborate this opinion. All I know is, that he would answer our signals each time they were sounded, to the infinite merriment of our men, who would respond with shouts of laughter each time he sounded his horn.

The course of the river could be discerned eastwardly at least a dozen miles, and there were several of the enemy's villages in that direction. We could see them approaching all the afternoon, in parties of from five to fifty, and it was estimated that there were at least three thousand Indians opposed to us,—more than ten to one. During the afternoon, parties of the enemy could be seen at a distance of two or three miles on either side, going to the village that we passed through in the morning, and they succeeded in getting all the stock that they had left, in securing such valuables as had been left by them in their lodges, and they also secured their women and children and carried them to places of safety.

The safety of our own wagon train now began to be considered, as there were only seventy-five men left with it, and it was feared that it might be captured by the large number of Indians that had passed to our rear. The most of our officers were anxious to press on and capture the village immediately in our front, and Carson was at one time about to give orders to that effect, when our Indians prevailed upon him to return and completely destroy the village that we had already captured, and after finding our supply train, replenishing our ammunition, and leaving our wounded, we could come back again and finish this village to our satisfaction.

After some hesitation and against the wishes of most of his officers, at about half-past three Carson gave orders to bring out the cavalry horses, and formed a column of fours,—the number four man of each set of fours to lead the other three horses,— with the mountain howitzers to bring up the rear of the column. The balance of the command was thrown out as skirmishers on the front, rear and on both flanks, and we commenced our return march. The enemy was not disposed to allow us to return without molestation, and in a very few minutes was attacking us on every side. By setting fire to the high, dry grass of the river bottom they drove us to the foothills, and by riding in rear of the tire as it came burning towards us, they would occasionally get within a few yards of the column; being enveloped in the smoke, they would deliver the fire of their rifles and get out of harm's way before they could be discovered by us.

During the morning's fight at the Adobe Walls, a young Mexican boy, about eighteen or nineteen years of age, belonging to one of the New Mexico companies, was out on the line of skirmishers, and as he was crawling forward, in reaching out his right hand he placed it over the hole of a rattlesnake and was bitten on the little finger. He passed near me, as he came away from the line to find the surgeon, and as he was holding up his hand, I supposed that he was wounded in that member, and said to him in Spanish, "*Que hay! que tienes?*"—"Here you, what's the matter?"

He replied "*Una bibora!*"—"rattlesnake."

He passed into the Adobe Walls, where the surgeon was located, who dressed his hand and gave him a good stiff drink of whisky. In a few minutes he returned to the skirmish line, where he remained until our return. His company was now on our left flank, and after we had completed about a mile of our return march, a Comanche rode up to us in a cloud of smoke, when a sudden gust of wind left him completely exposed within twenty feet of the boy who had been bitten by the snake. They both, at the same moment, brought their rifles to their cheeks. The Indian fired a second before the other, and missed his mark,—the boy immediately returned the fire, hit his enemy in some vital part, (he instantly fell from off his horse,) and rushed forward to secure his scalp.

Some ten or fifteen of the Comanches who were near, saw their friend fall and rushed forward on their horses to secure the body and bear it away out of our reach, as they had done a great many times during the day. The comrades of the Mexican soldier went to his assistance, kept the enemy at bay until he had finished the scalping operation, and then returned to their places in the skirmish line. This boy took the only scalp that our party secured during the whole day's fight. During this return march the howitzer in rear of the column succeeded in getting in a shell three several times on groups of the enemy.

Just before sundown we reached the village, which we found

full of Indians trying to save their property from destruction. A couple of shells, followed by a charge of our men, drove them into the far end of it, when the work of destruction commenced, about half of the command being detailed to set tire to the lodges, while the rest of us were to keep the enemy in check. A small sand hill about twenty feet high was taken advantage of for the howitzer, and served as earthworks for the detachment. The pieces were loaded at the foot of the hill, and at the command of "By hand, to the front," they were pushed to the top. when the gunner would aim the piece, and at the command "ready" number four would insert the friction primer, and lying on his stomach, with no part of his body exposed, would wait for the command to fire.

The piece on being fired would recoil, sometimes tumbling over and over and at others coming down fairly on the wheels to the bottom of the hill, when the other piece, having been loaded meanwhile, would be moved to the top and fired in its turn.

The lodges were found to be full of plunder, including many Hundreds of finely finished buffalo robes. Every man in the command took possession of one or more of these, while the balance were consumed in the lodges. There were found some white women's clothing, as well as articles of children's clothing, and several photographs; also a cavalry sergeant's hat, with letter and cross-sabres, cavalry sabre and belts, etc., being the accoutrements of the Colorado volunteer sergeant of which I have spoken before. We also burned an army ambulance and government wagon, with several sets of harnesses, which the Kiowas had retained from some wagon train they had captured during the previous summer.

I had forgotten to mention that with our seventy-two Utes and Apaches there were two old squaws, and the purpose for which they had accompanied the party had been a mystery to our men, but we ascertained now. It is well known to all frontiersmen that the mutilation of dead bodies (and they are often found mutilated so indecently that I cannot describe it here—a dozen time or more I have been eye-witness to this kind of mu-

CAPTAIN GEORGE H. PETTIS,
First Regiment of Infantry, California Volunteers,
who commanded a battery of Howitzers in the Indian
fight at Adobe Walls, Texas, November 25, 1864.

tilation myself,) is always the work of the squaws.

When we passed the village in the morning, these two squaws were in these lodges, unknown to us, seeking for plunder. In the course of their search, they had found two old, decrepit, blind Kiowas and two cripples, who were unable to get out of their lodges when they were deserted by their people, and our two squaws soon placed them *hors-du-combat*, by cleaving their heads with axes. All four of these were found by our men when they were burning the village, the squaws themselves showing the men where they were, and claiming the merit of their slaughter.

The Comanches and Kiowas were driven from lodge to lodge to the southern extremity of the village, and on reaching the last one, the party, numbering some thirty or forty, mounted their horses, and. at a run made from us towards the river, a twelve-pounder shell, the last shot fired in the fight, exploding in their midst, as a parting salute, just as the sun was setting in the western horizon. The work of destruction was soon finished,— every one of the one hundred and seventy-six lodges, with their contents, were consumed, together with the ambulance, wagon and harnesses before mentioned.

It was some time after dark when the cavalrymen had mounted their horses and had formed the column to return. The two gun carriages and the two ammunition carts were loaded with the most severely wounded, while the slightly wounded retained their horses. The march now became the most unpleasant part of the day's operations. The wounded were suffering severely; the men and horses were completely worn out; the enemy might attack us at any moment, unseen; and the uncertainty of the whereabouts and condition of our wagon train, for you will remember that we were now nearly two hundred and fifty miles from the nearest habitation, or hopes of supply, with the whole Comanche and Kiowa nations at our heels,—all combined to make it anything but a pleasant situation to be in.

We had been moving slowly on our return from the destroyed village about three hours, when we saw away off on our right several camp fires burning dimly, and approaching cautiously, we were soon welcomed by the challenge of a sentinel, in good, clear, ringing Saxon, "Who comes there?" This was answered by our men with cheers, for we were now assured that our supply train was intact, and that starvation would be averted for a season at least. But a few minutes elapsed be fore we were in camp, the Surgeon made the wounded as comfortable as possible, the horses were unsaddled and unhitched from the pieces and fastened to the picket line, a double guard was put on, and then for blankets and sleep, hunger being forgotten in our weariness.

This ended the day's work. The command had been nearly thirty hours marching and fighting, with an intermission of less than half an hour, and with no other refreshment than that afforded by a single hard-bread, and small piece of salt pork. The casualties of the day on our part were but two killed, privates John O'Donnell and John Sullivan, of Company M, First California Cavalry, with twenty-one wounded, two or three of whom died afterwards from the effects of their wounds. One of our Utes was killed and four wounded.

The loss to the Comanches and Kiowas, was, their village of one hundred and seventy-six lodges, buffalo robes, and all of their Winter's provisions, with nearly one hundred killed, and between one hundred and one hundred and fifty wounded. There were three officers, Major William McCleave, and Capt. Emil Fritz. Co. B, 1st California Cavalry, and Lieut. Geo. H. Pettis, 1st California Infantry and sixty-six men who belonged to the "California Column," that participated in this action.

Our wagon train had left camp at Mule Creek very early in the morning, had followed our trail as well as they could, and all day long had heard the howitzers each time they were fired. They knew that we were engaged with the enemy, and the train was kept in continuous motion, hoping to reach us before the day closed; but night set in on them, and Colonel Abreú selected a good place for defence and went into camp where we found them, they not having been molested by the Indians, although several parties were seen by them during the day.

As the usual time for an Indian attack is just before daybreak, reveille was sounded at an early hour on the morning of the twenty-sixth, the command was distributed for an attack, but the sun soon rose upon us awaiting the onset. As none of the enemy were discovered, the officers and men, now that they had been refreshed by undisturbed slumber, bethought themselves of their stomachs, and I doubt if there was ever a heartier breakfast disposed of; all of the wild turkeys and antelope meat on hand were devoured,—calling upon the hunters to do their duty again. Our Indians were so tired the night before that they adjourned their "scalp dance," and sought the comfort of their buffalo robes; but, as we had been entertained every night until the fight by their "war dance," so for twenty-one days after, or as long as they remained with us, the monotony of the march was diversified by their own peculiar "scalp dance," and that with only one scalp, which they had purchased of the Mexican soldier whose exploit I have before mentioned.

We remained in camp during the day to allow the men and animals to recuperate, and never was needed rest more welcome. The enemy did not seem disposed to molest us, but remained in full view, on an eminence about two miles to the eastward of us. The only incident of the day worthy of mention was, that during the afternoon two of our Indians, mounted rode out leisurely on the plain towards the Comanches; presently two of the enemy left their party and rode towards us, when another party of ten or a dozen left our camp, and then the same number left the camp of the enemy, like boys playing at goal, and then another party from our camp, followed by a like party from the enemy, until there were over two hundred men of both sides moving at a walk towards each other in the centre of the plain.

The leading parties of each side had approached each other until only about two hundred yards of space intervened, when shooting commenced, but before a dozen shots had been exchanged the entire body of the enemy turned their horses' heads towards their camp, and left on a run, followed by our people for a short distance, who afterwards returned to camp unharmed.

Reveille was sounded early on the morning of the twenty-seventh, and after breakfast orders were issued by Colonel Carson to saddle up, and commence the return march, much to the surprise and dissatisfaction of all the officers, who desired to go to the Comanche village that we had been in sight of on the day of the fight. It was learned afterwards that our Indians had advised Carson to return, and without consulting his officers the order was given and we commenced our return march.

We arrived at Fort Bascom on or about the twentieth of December without being molested by the enemy, where we remained a few days, when orders were received from the Department Commander for the different detachments to return to various posts in the Territory, and as the term of enlistment of the most of the men of my detachment had expired, I was ordered to Fort Union, where we arrived shortly after, on New Year's day, 1865.

General Orders, No. 4, Department of New Mexico, dated Headquarters, Santa Fé, N. M., February 18, 1865, which gives a detailed account of every operation with the Indians in that department for the entire year of 1864, says, on page 10, under date of November twenty-fifth:

Colonel Christopher Carson, First Cavalry, New Mexico Volunteers, with a command consisting of fourteen commissioned officers and three hundred and twenty-one enlisted men and seventy-five Indians,—Apaches and Utes—attacked a Kiowa village of about one hundred and fifty lodges, near the Adobe Fort, on the Canadian River, in Texas; and, after a severe fight, compelled the Indians to retreat, with a loss of sixty killed and wounded. The village was then destroyed. The engagement commenced at 8:30 a. m., and lasted without intermission until sunset.

In this fight, privates John O'Donnell and John Sullivan, of Company M, First Cavalry, California Volunteers, were killed, and Corporal N. Newman, privates Thomas Briggs, J. Jamison, —— Mapes, Jaspar Vincent and J. Horsley, of Company B, Sergeant John M. Nelson, Co., K., 1st California Cavalry, was badly wounded, and Sergeant Nelson was badly wounded and had his leg amputated at the upper third of the thigh. He is now a resident of Ford City, Penn., and —— Holygrapher, of Company G, First Cavalry, California Volunteers, Antonio Duro and Antonio Qauches, of Company M, and H. Romero, of Company I, First Cavalry. New Mexico Volunteers, were wounded. Four Utes were wounded.

Colonel Carson, in his report mentions the following officers as deserving the highest praise: Major McCleave, Captain Fritz and Lieutenant Heath, of the First Cavalry, California Volunteers; Captains Deus and Berney, First Cavalry, New Mexico Volunteers; Lieutenant Pettis, First Infantry, California Volunteers: Lieutenant Edgar, First Cavalry, New Mexico Volunteers, and Assistant Surgeon George T. Courtright, United States Volunteers.

The command destroyed one hundred and fifty lodges of the best manufacture, a large amount of dried meats, berries, buffalo robes, powder, cooking utensils, etc., also, a buggy and spring wagon, the property of 'Sierrito,' or 'Little Mountain,' the Kiowa Chief.

In 1867, about three years after the events narrated here, I was residing in a little Mexican village on the Rio Grande, Los Algodones, about forty-five miles south of Santa Fé, where I became acquainted with a couple of Mexicans who were trading with the Comanche and Kiowa Indians in the fall of 1864, and they informed me that they were at the Comanche village which we were in sight of, and that when the fight commenced they were held as prisoners and kept so for several days after we left that neighbourhood; that in the village on the day of the fight there were seven white women and several white children, prisoners; they also informed me where the women and. children of the village were hid when we passed through the Kiowa village on the morning of the fight, and that our enemy sustained a loss on that day, of nearly a hundred killed and between one hundred and one hundred and fifty wounded, making a difference with the official report, which guessed at thirty killed and thirty wounded.

They also said that the Indians claimed that if the whites had not had with them the two "guns that shot twice," referring to the shells of the mountain howitzers, they would never have allowed a single white man to escape out of the valley of the Canadian, and I may say, with becoming modesty, that this was also the often expressed opinion of Colonel Carson.

www.ingramcontent.com/pod-product-compliance
Lightning Source LLC
Chambersburg PA
CBHW031902090426
42741CB00005B/608